Date: 7/12/18

sky·doll

Sudra

TITAN
COMICS

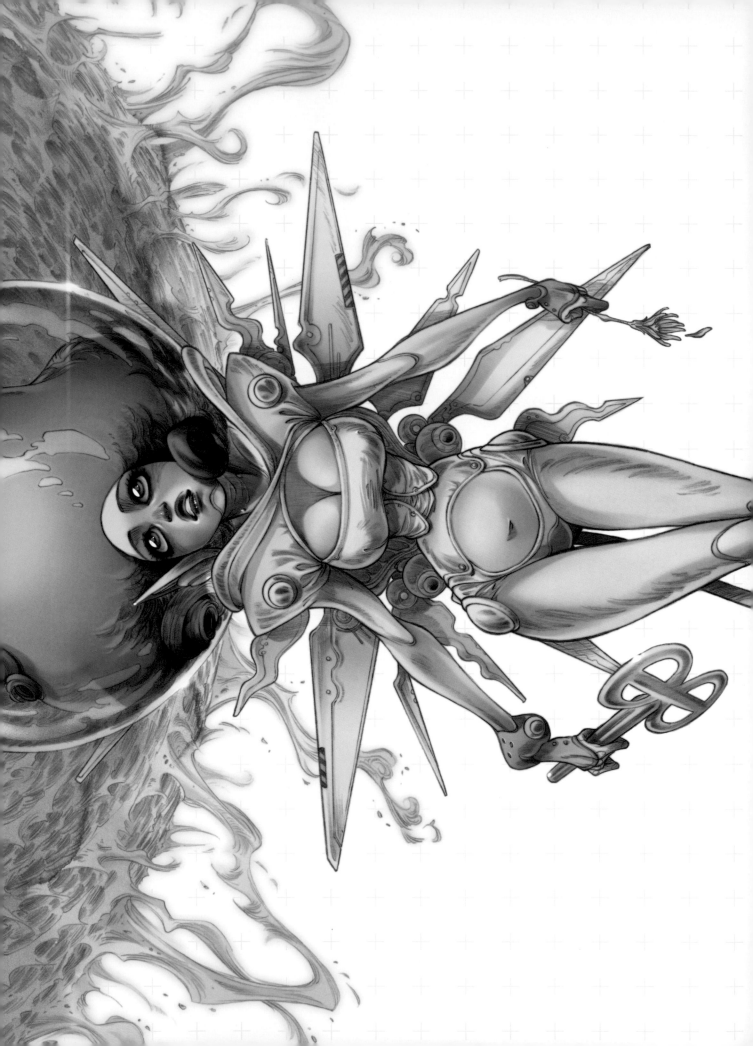

Do you think androids have a soul?

Philip K. Dick

sky·doll

Sudra

On the planet Sudra, all the religions throughout the
known universe are practiced, creating a paradise of tolerance
and freedom. For Noa, this freedom means a chance at a new start,
as she performs minor miracles in the street, allowing her to scrape a
living. She may finally be free from outside control – but she's keeping
secrets from those she loves. When she realizes trouble is coming, her
past comes back to haunt her, and she is forced to face the
truth about who, and what, she really is...

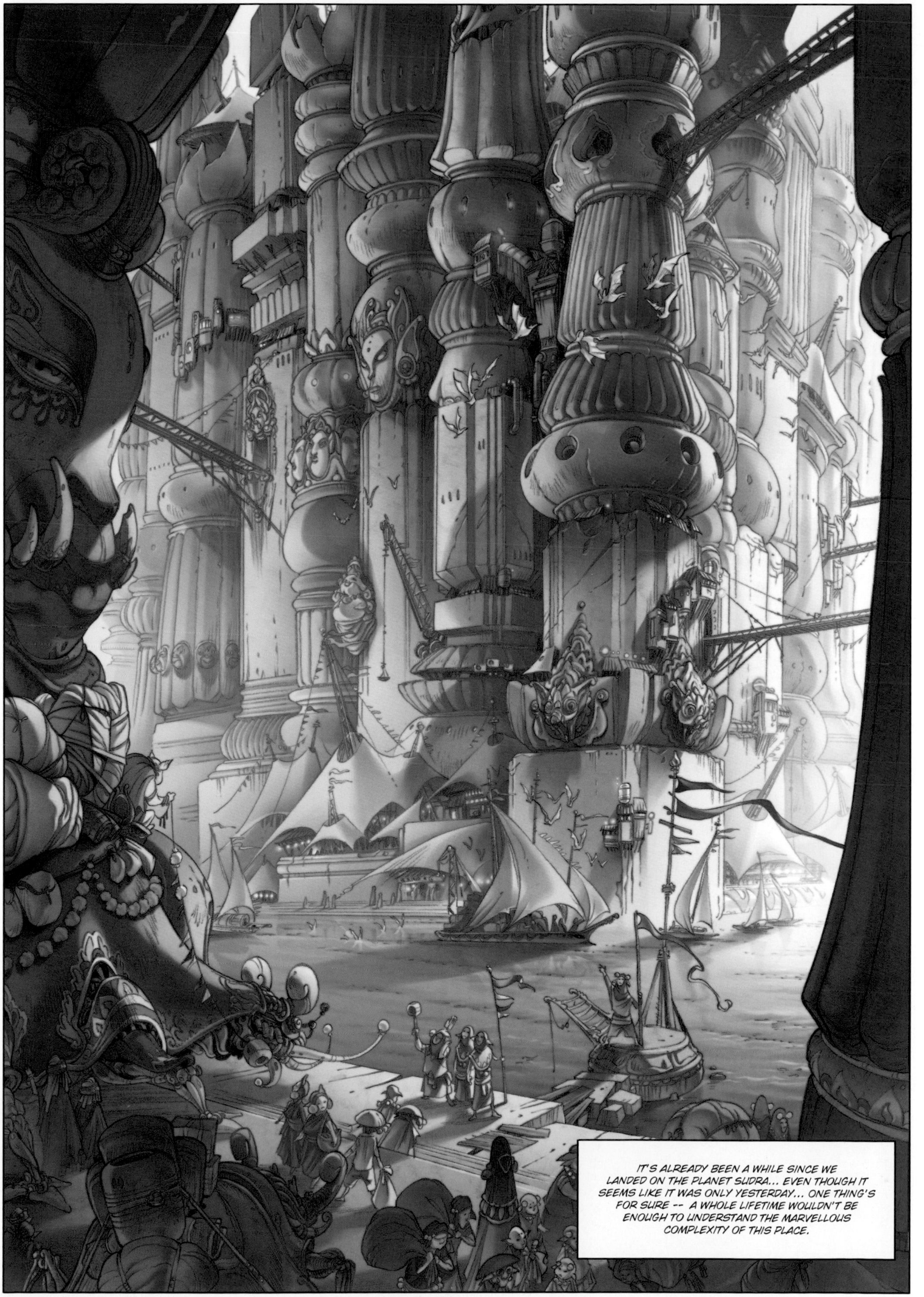
IT'S ALREADY BEEN A WHILE SINCE WE LANDED ON THE PLANET SUDRA... EVEN THOUGH IT SEEMS LIKE IT WAS ONLY YESTERDAY... ONE THING'S FOR SURE -- A WHOLE LIFETIME WOULDN'T BE ENOUGH TO UNDERSTAND THE MARVELLOUS COMPLEXITY OF THIS PLACE.

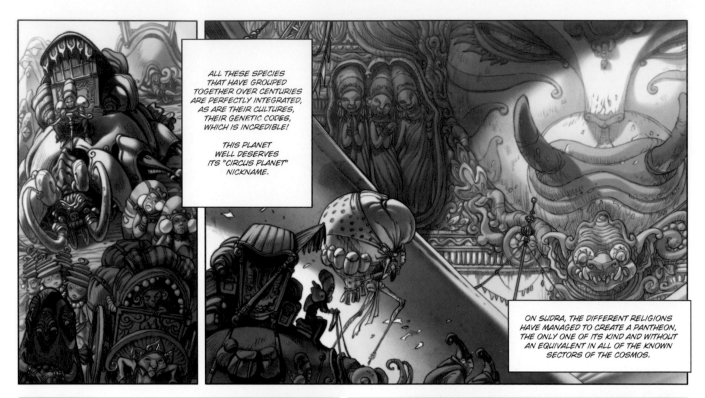

ALL THESE SPECIES THAT HAVE GROUPED TOGETHER OVER CENTURIES ARE PERFECTLY INTEGRATED, AS ARE THEIR CULTURES, THEIR GENETIC CODES, WHICH IS INCREDIBLE!

THIS PLANET WELL DESERVES ITS "CIRCUS PLANET" NICKNAME.

ON SUDRA, THE DIFFERENT RELIGIONS HAVE MANAGED TO CREATE A PANTHEON, THE ONLY ONE OF ITS KIND AND WITHOUT AN EQUIVALENT IN ALL OF THE KNOWN SECTORS OF THE COSMOS.

IT'S AN IMPENETRABLE JUNGLE THAT I TRY EVERY DAY, IN VAIN, TO EXPLORE.

THOUSANDS OF ANCIENT AND NEW DIVINITIES EXIST SIDE-BY-SIDE. EACH ONE AMONG THEM POSSESSES DOZENS, MAYBE EVEN HUNDREDS OF VARIOUS NAMES AND INTERPRETATIONS.

UNDER THEIR STONY EYES, THE CITY IS RUMBLING, NOISY, AND CHAOTIC...

...AND OFTEN CRUEL, CREATING SEVERE DIFFERENCES ALONG WITH ENORMOUS SOCIAL DISPARITY.

THE PEACEFUL WATERS OF ITS CANALS ARE NO MORE THAN A MIRROR OF THE PLANET...

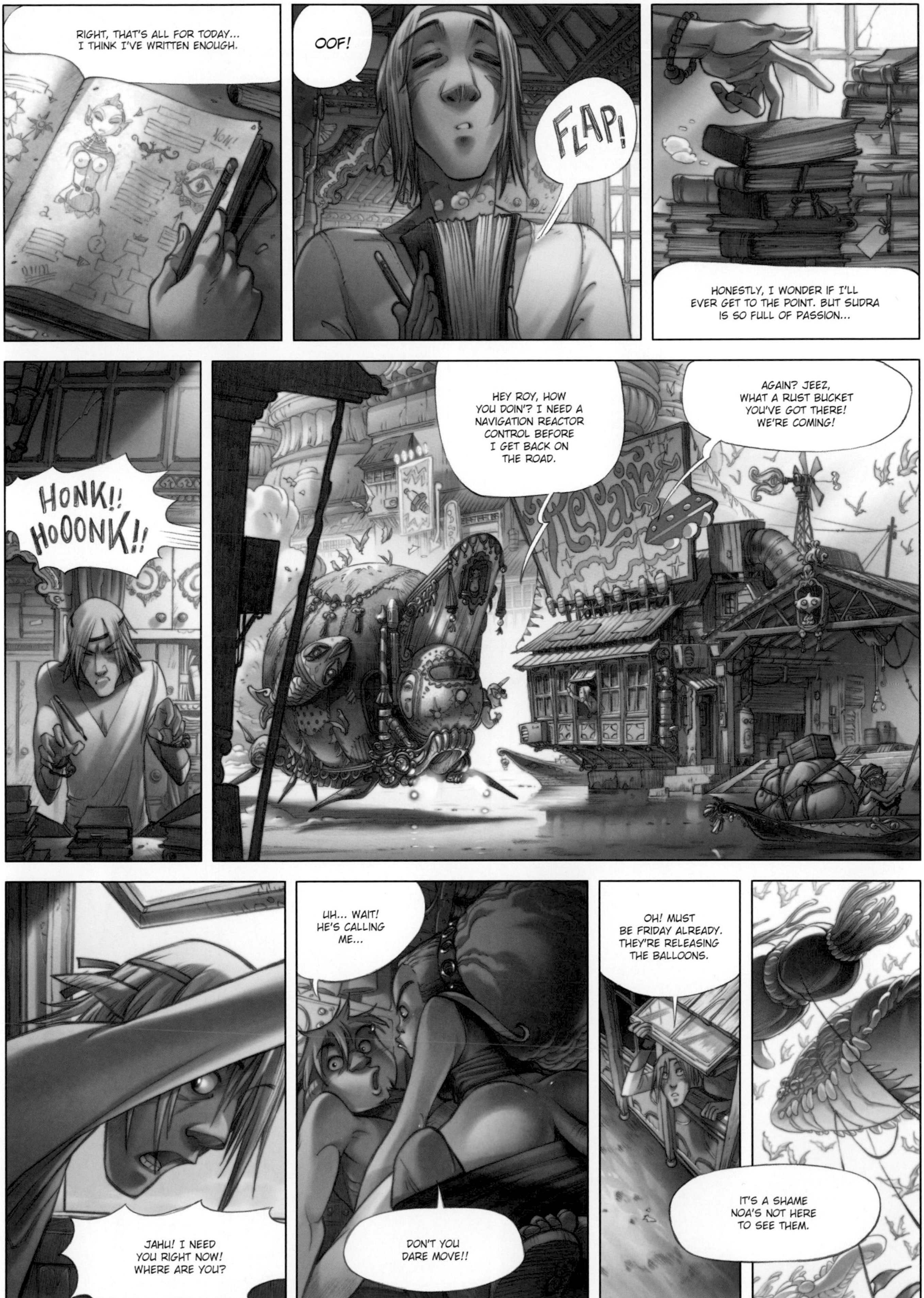
RIGHT, THAT'S ALL FOR TODAY... I THINK I'VE WRITTEN ENOUGH.
OOF!
FLAP!
HONESTLY, I WONDER IF I'LL EVER GET TO THE POINT. BUT SUDRA IS SO FULL OF PASSION...
HONK!! HoOONK!!
HEY ROY, HOW YOU DOIN'? I NEED A NAVIGATION REACTOR CONTROL BEFORE I GET BACK ON THE ROAD.
AGAIN? JEEZ, WHAT A RUST BUCKET YOU'VE GOT THERE! WE'RE COMING!
JAHU! I NEED YOU RIGHT NOW! WHERE ARE YOU?
UH... WAIT! HE'S CALLING ME...
DON'T YOU DARE MOVE!!
OH! MUST BE FRIDAY ALREADY. THEY'RE RELEASING THE BALLOONS.
IT'S A SHAME NOA'S NOT HERE TO SEE THEM.

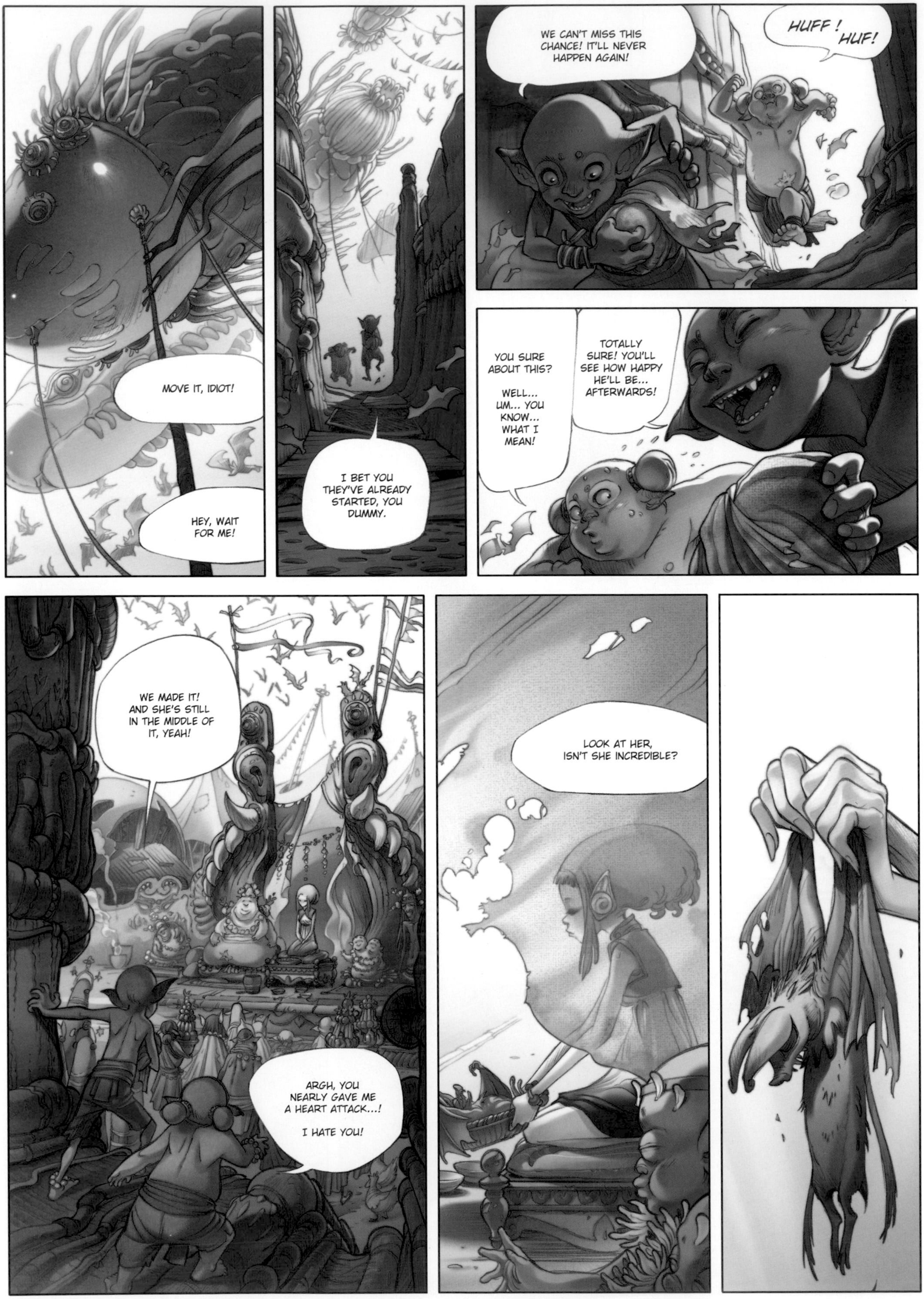
MOVE IT, IDIOT!
HEY, WAIT FOR ME!
I BET YOU THEY'VE ALREADY STARTED, YOU DUMMY.
WE CAN'T MISS THIS CHANCE! IT'LL NEVER HAPPEN AGAIN!
HUFF! HUF!
YOU SURE ABOUT THIS?
WELL... UM... YOU KNOW... WHAT I MEAN!
TOTALLY SURE! YOU'LL SEE HOW HAPPY HE'LL BE... AFTERWARDS!
WE MADE IT! AND SHE'S STILL IN THE MIDDLE OF IT, YEAH!
ARGH, YOU NEARLY GAVE ME A HEART ATTACK...! I HATE YOU!
LOOK AT HER, ISN'T SHE INCREDIBLE?

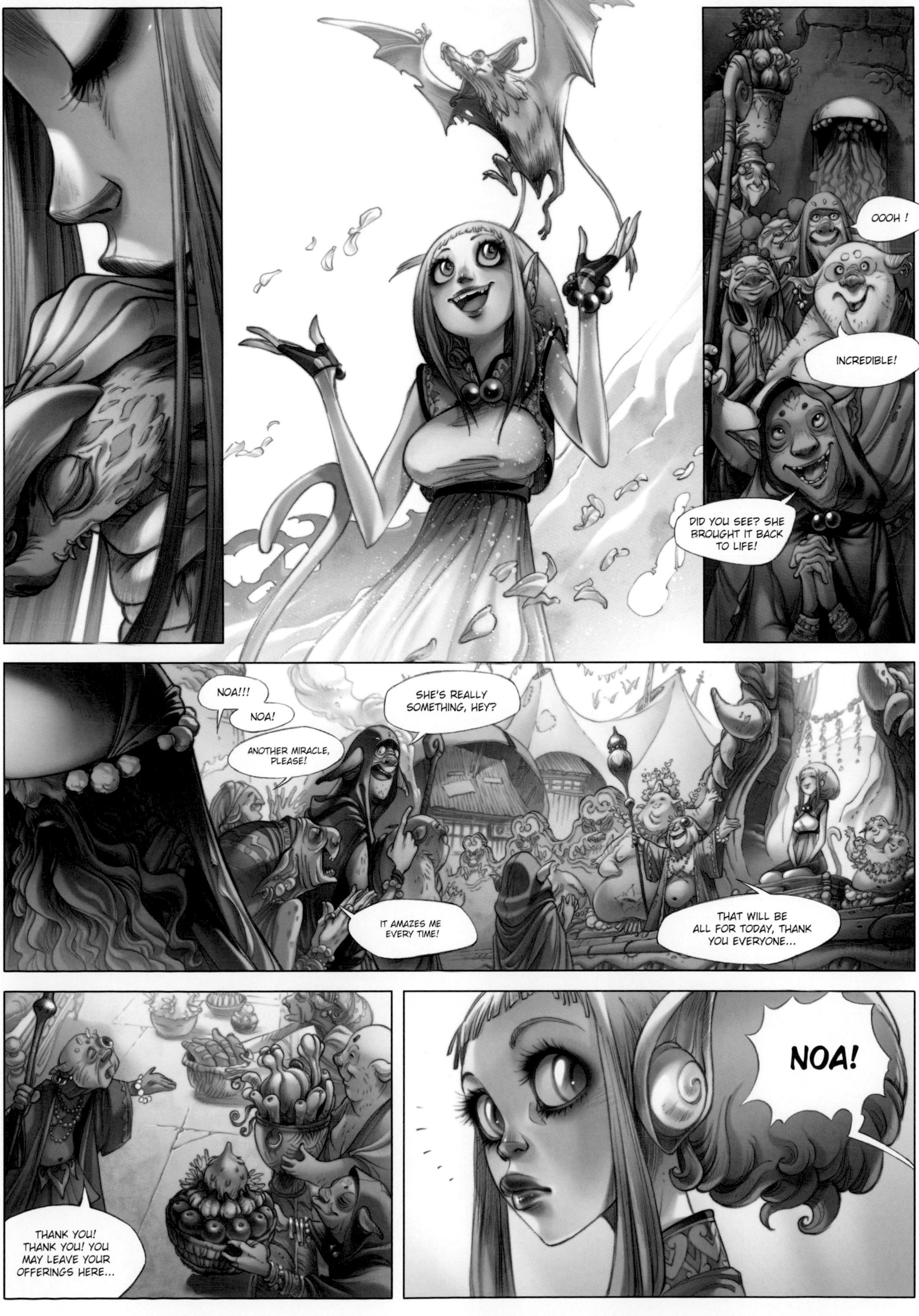
OOOH !
INCREDIBLE!
DID YOU SEE? SHE BROUGHT IT BACK TO LIFE!
NOA!!!
NOA!
SHE'S REALLY SOMETHING, HEY?
ANOTHER MIRACLE, PLEASE!
IT AMAZES ME EVERY TIME!
THAT WILL BE ALL FOR TODAY, THANK YOU EVERYONE...
THANK YOU! THANK YOU! YOU MAY LEAVE YOUR OFFERINGS HERE...
NOA!

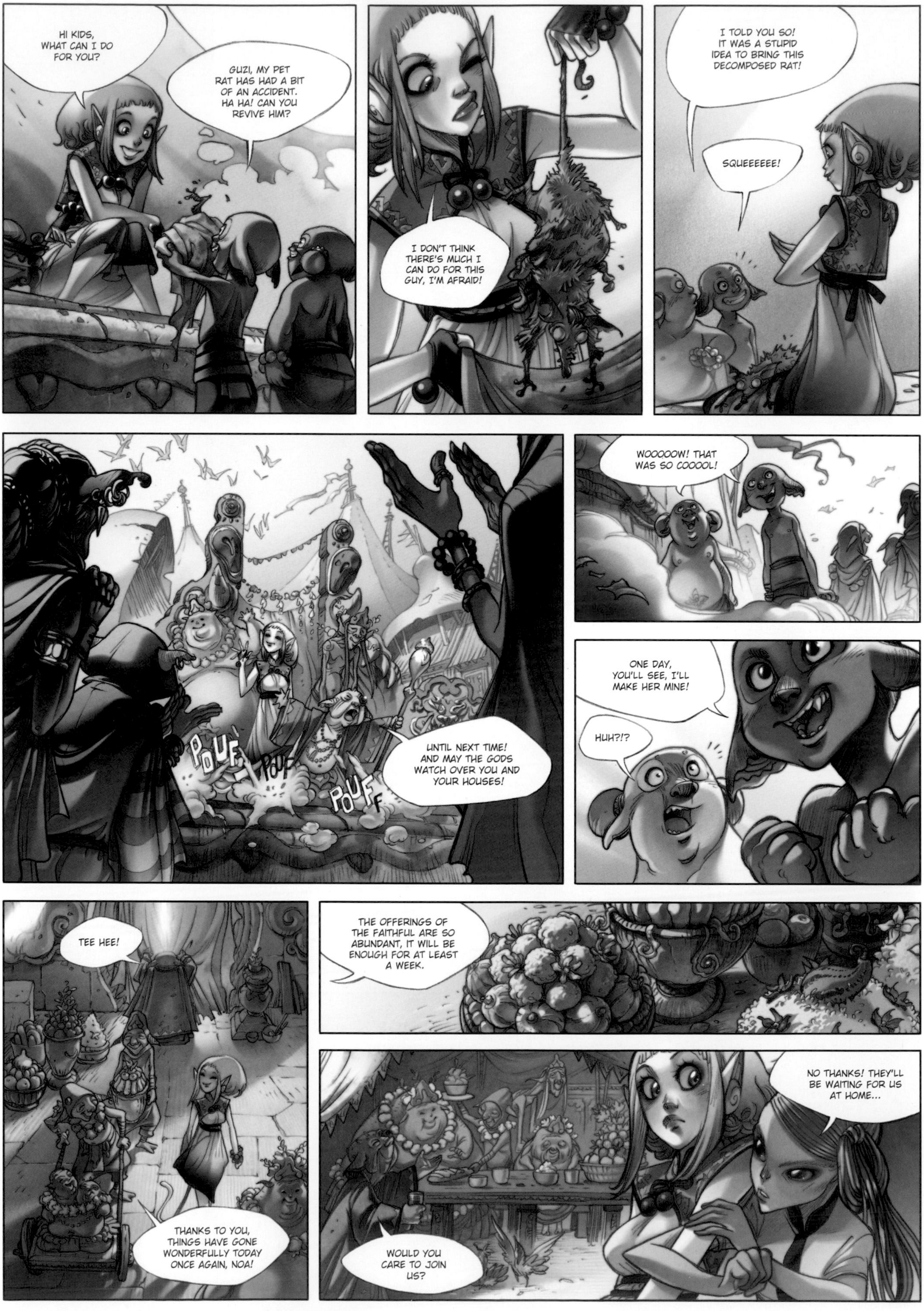
HI KIDS, WHAT CAN I DO FOR YOU?
GUZI, MY PET RAT HAS HAD A BIT OF AN ACCIDENT. HA HA! CAN YOU REVIVE HIM?
I DON'T THINK THERE'S MUCH I CAN DO FOR THIS GUY, I'M AFRAID!
I TOLD YOU SO! IT WAS A STUPID IDEA TO BRING THIS DECOMPOSED RAT!
SQUEEEEEE!
POUF
POUF
POUFF
UNTIL NEXT TIME! AND MAY THE GODS WATCH OVER YOU AND YOUR HOUSES!
WOOOOOW! THAT WAS SO COOOOL!
ONE DAY, YOU'LL SEE, I'LL MAKE HER MINE!
HUH?!?
TEE HEE!
THANKS TO YOU, THINGS HAVE GONE WONDERFULLY TODAY ONCE AGAIN, NOA!
THE OFFERINGS OF THE FAITHFUL ARE SO ABUNDANT, IT WILL BE ENOUGH FOR AT LEAST A WEEK.
WOULD YOU CARE TO JOIN US?
NO THANKS! THEY'LL BE WAITING FOR US AT HOME...

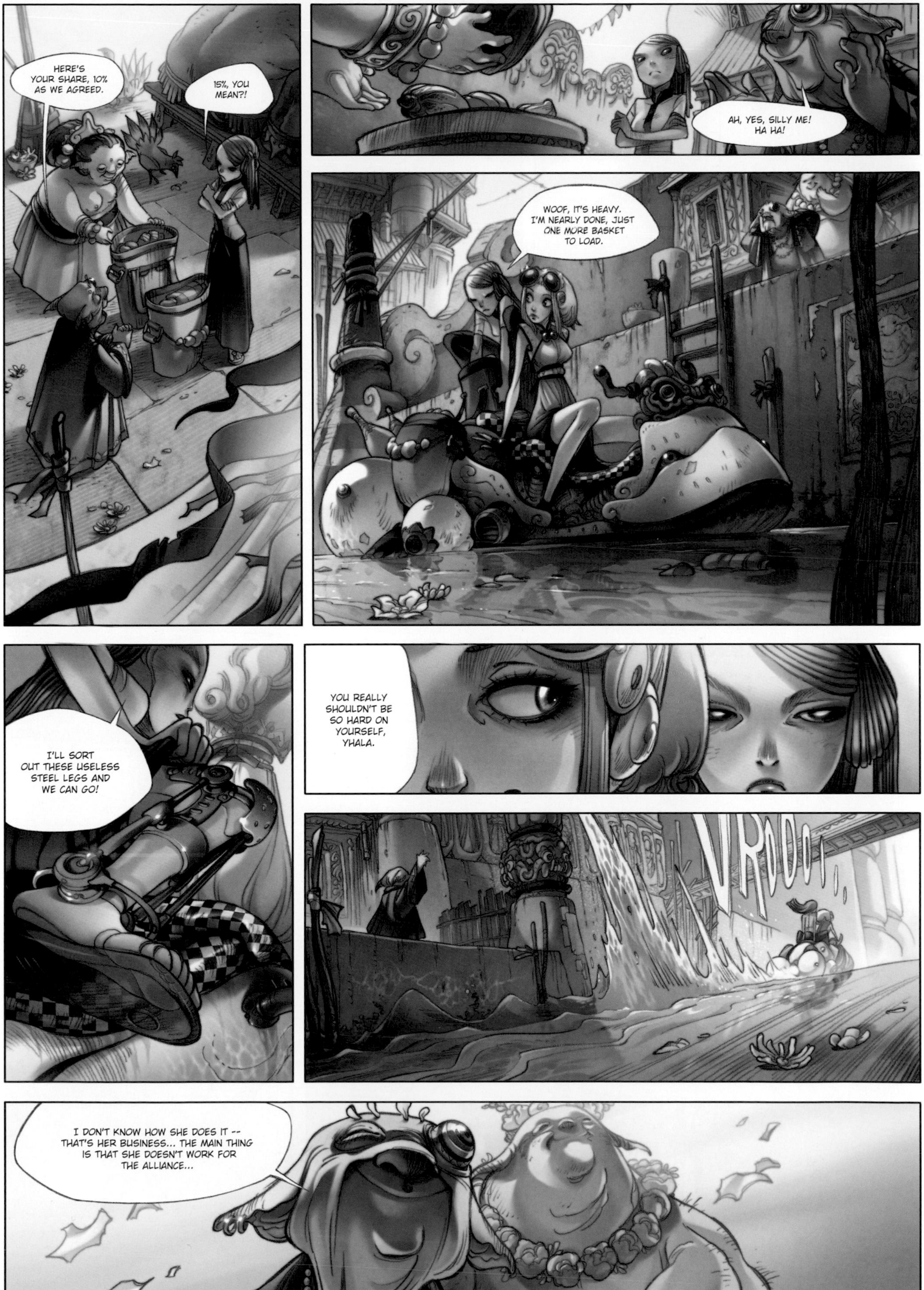
HERE'S YOUR SHARE, 10% AS WE AGREED.
15%, YOU MEAN?!
AH, YES, SILLY ME! HA HA!
WOOF, IT'S HEAVY. I'M NEARLY DONE, JUST ONE MORE BASKET TO LOAD.
I'LL SORT OUT THESE USELESS STEEL LEGS AND WE CAN GO!
YOU REALLY SHOULDN'T BE SO HARD ON YOURSELF, YHALA.
VROOO
I DON'T KNOW HOW SHE DOES IT -- THAT'S HER BUSINESS... THE MAIN THING IS THAT SHE DOESN'T WORK FOR THE ALLIANCE...

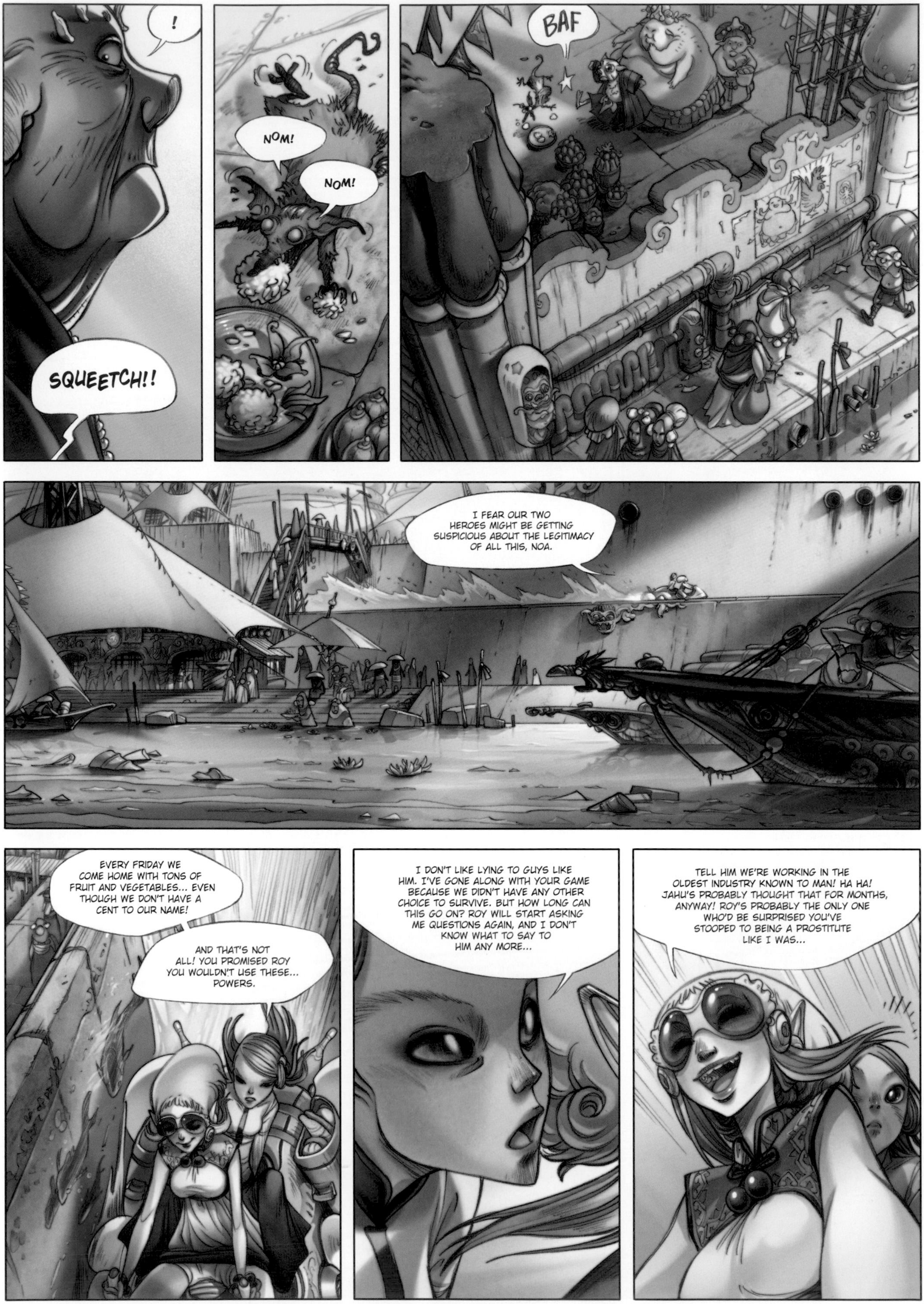
!
SQUEETCH!!
NOM!
NOM!
BAF
I FEAR OUR TWO HEROES MIGHT BE GETTING SUSPICIOUS ABOUT THE LEGITIMACY OF ALL THIS, NOA.
EVERY FRIDAY WE COME HOME WITH TONS OF FRUIT AND VEGETABLES... EVEN THOUGH WE DON'T HAVE A CENT TO OUR NAME!
AND THAT'S NOT ALL! YOU PROMISED ROY YOU WOULDN'T USE THESE... POWERS.
I DON'T LIKE LYING TO GUYS LIKE HIM. I'VE GONE ALONG WITH YOUR GAME BECAUSE WE DIDN'T HAVE ANY OTHER CHOICE TO SURVIVE. BUT HOW LONG CAN THIS GO ON? ROY WILL START ASKING ME QUESTIONS AGAIN, AND I DON'T KNOW WHAT TO SAY TO HIM ANY MORE...
TELL HIM WE'RE WORKING IN THE OLDEST INDUSTRY KNOWN TO MAN! HA HA! JAHU'S PROBABLY THOUGHT THAT FOR MONTHS, ANYWAY! ROY'S PROBABLY THE ONLY ONE WHO'D BE SURPRISED YOU'VE STOOPED TO BEING A PROSTITUTE LIKE I WAS...

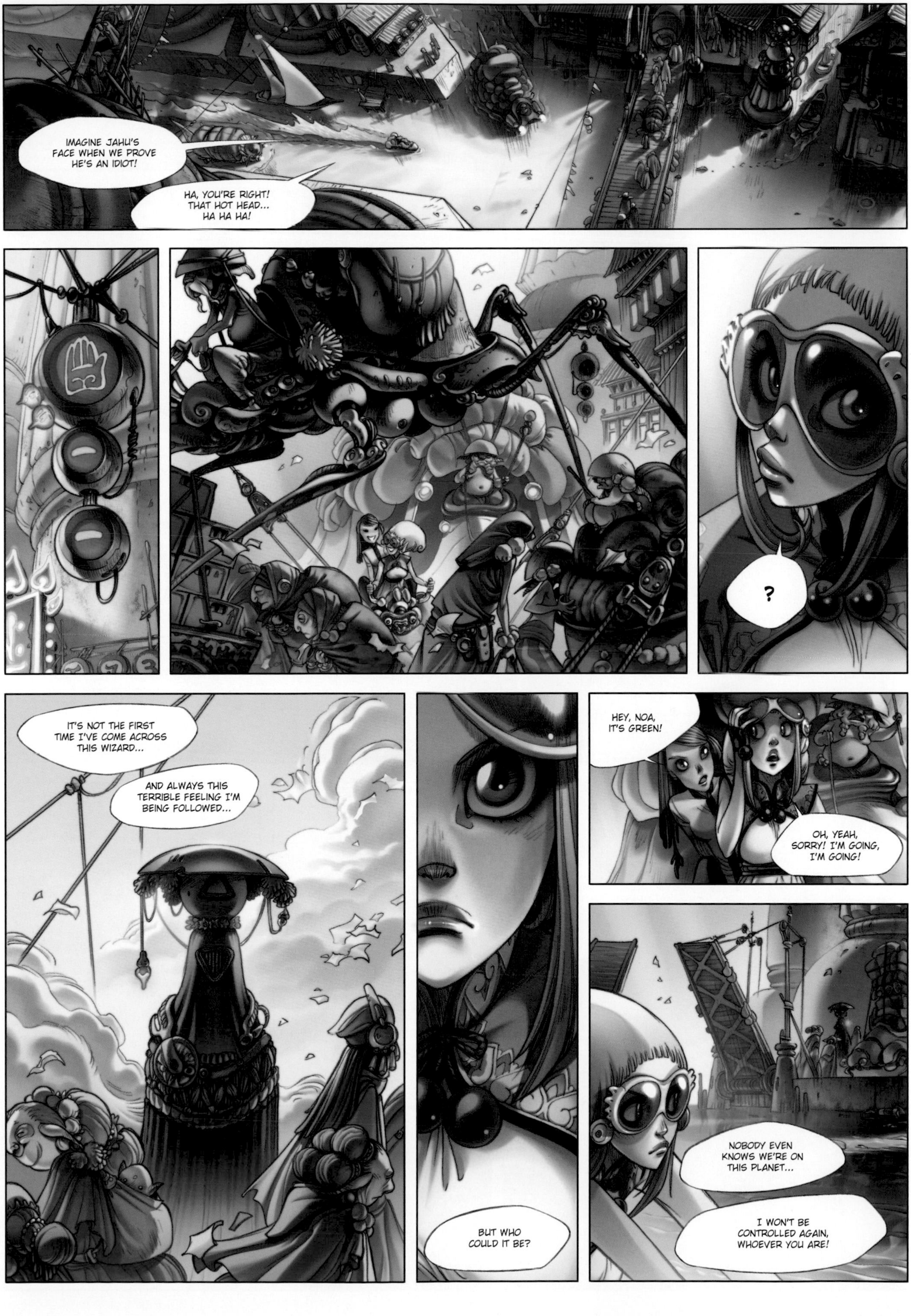
IMAGINE JAHU'S FACE WHEN WE PROVE HE'S AN IDIOT!
HA, YOU'RE RIGHT! THAT HOT HEAD... HA HA HA!
?
IT'S NOT THE FIRST TIME I'VE COME ACROSS THIS WIZARD...
AND ALWAYS THIS TERRIBLE FEELING I'M BEING FOLLOWED...
BUT WHO COULD IT BE?
HEY, NOA, IT'S GREEN!
OH, YEAH, SORRY! I'M GOING, I'M GOING!
NOBODY EVEN KNOWS WE'RE ON THIS PLANET...
I WON'T BE CONTROLLED AGAIN, WHOEVER YOU ARE!

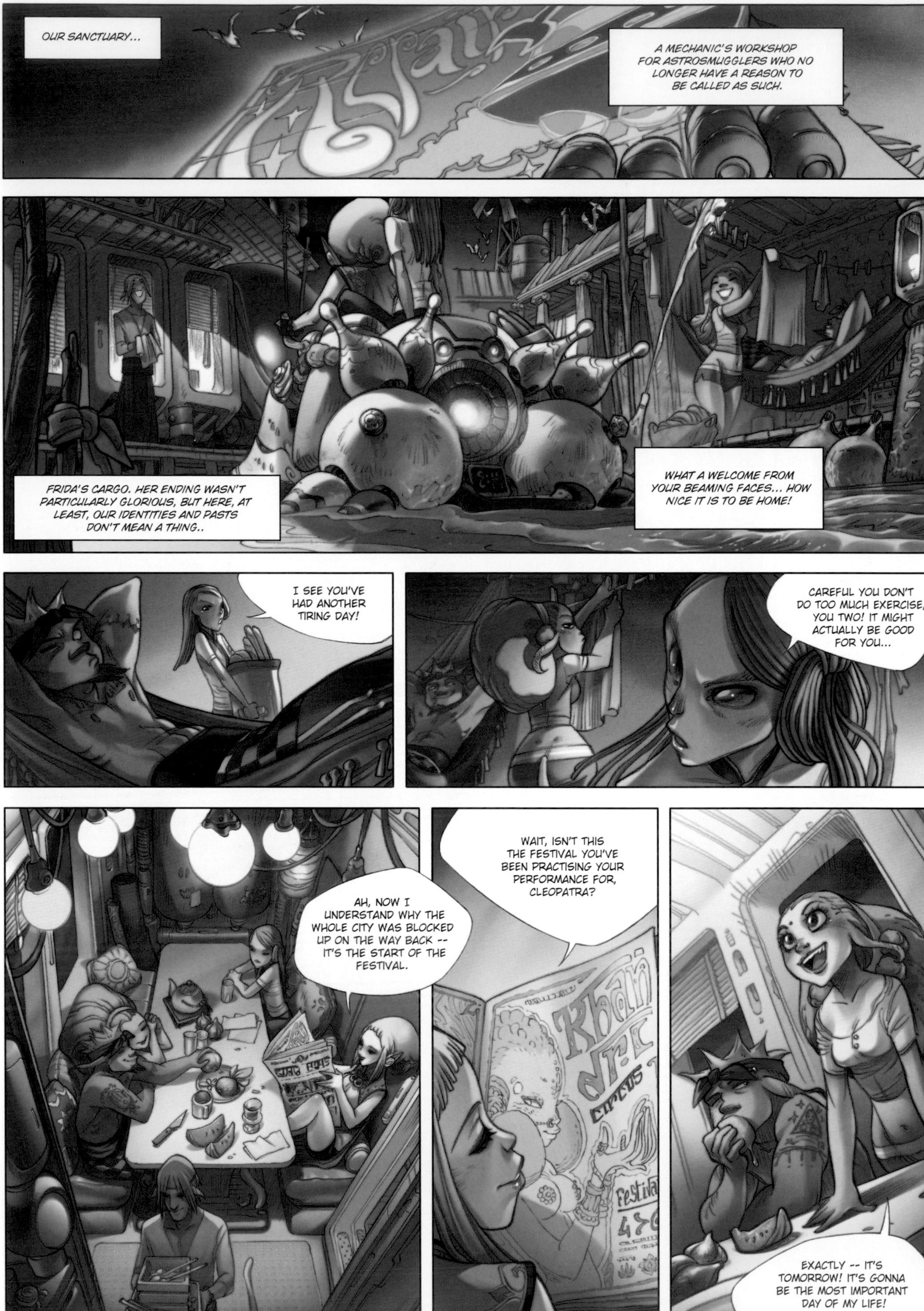
OUR SANCTUARY...
A MECHANIC'S WORKSHOP FOR ASTROSMUGGLERS WHO NO LONGER HAVE A REASON TO BE CALLED AS SUCH.
FRIDA'S CARGO. HER ENDING WASN'T PARTICULARLY GLORIOUS, BUT HERE, AT LEAST, OUR IDENTITIES AND PASTS DON'T MEAN A THING..
WHAT A WELCOME FROM YOUR BEAMING FACES... HOW NICE IT IS TO BE HOME!
I SEE YOU'VE HAD ANOTHER TIRING DAY!
CAREFUL YOU DON'T DO TOO MUCH EXERCISE, YOU TWO! IT MIGHT ACTUALLY BE GOOD FOR YOU...
AH, NOW I UNDERSTAND WHY THE WHOLE CITY WAS BLOCKED UP ON THE WAY BACK -- IT'S THE START OF THE FESTIVAL.
WAIT, ISN'T THIS THE FESTIVAL YOU'VE BEEN PRACTISING YOUR PERFORMANCE FOR, CLEOPATRA?
EXACTLY -- IT'S TOMORROW! IT'S GONNA BE THE MOST IMPORTANT DAY OF MY LIFE!

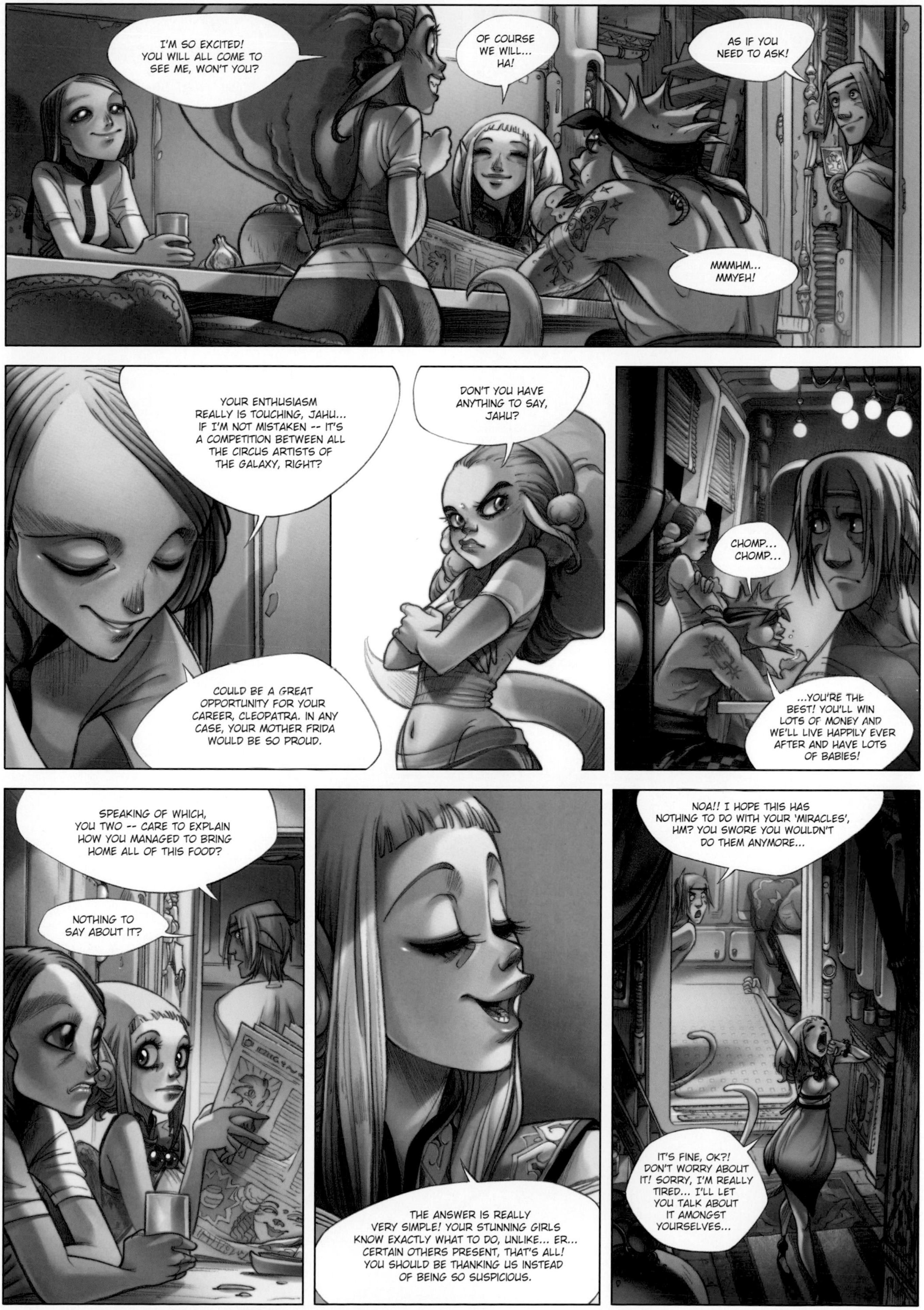
I'M SO EXCITED! YOU WILL ALL COME TO SEE ME, WON'T YOU?
OF COURSE WE WILL... HA!
AS IF YOU NEED TO ASK!
MMMHM... MMYEH!
YOUR ENTHUSIASM REALLY IS TOUCHING, JAHU... IF I'M NOT MISTAKEN -- IT'S A COMPETITION BETWEEN ALL THE CIRCUS ARTISTS OF THE GALAXY, RIGHT?
COULD BE A GREAT OPPORTUNITY FOR YOUR CAREER, CLEOPATRA. IN ANY CASE, YOUR MOTHER FRIDA WOULD BE SO PROUD.
DON'T YOU HAVE ANYTHING TO SAY, JAHU?
CHOMP... CHOMP...
...YOU'RE THE BEST! YOU'LL WIN LOTS OF MONEY AND WE'LL LIVE HAPPILY EVER AFTER AND HAVE LOTS OF BABIES!
SPEAKING OF WHICH, YOU TWO -- CARE TO EXPLAIN HOW YOU MANAGED TO BRING HOME ALL OF THIS FOOD?
NOTHING TO SAY ABOUT IT?
THE ANSWER IS REALLY VERY SIMPLE! YOUR STUNNING GIRLS KNOW EXACTLY WHAT TO DO, UNLIKE... ER... CERTAIN OTHERS PRESENT, THAT'S ALL! YOU SHOULD BE THANKING US INSTEAD OF BEING SO SUSPICIOUS.
NOA!! I HOPE THIS HAS NOTHING TO DO WITH YOUR 'MIRACLES', HM? YOU SWORE YOU WOULDN'T DO THEM ANYMORE...
IT'S FINE, OK?! DON'T WORRY ABOUT IT! SORRY, I'M REALLY TIRED... I'LL LET YOU TALK ABOUT IT AMONGST YOURSELVES...

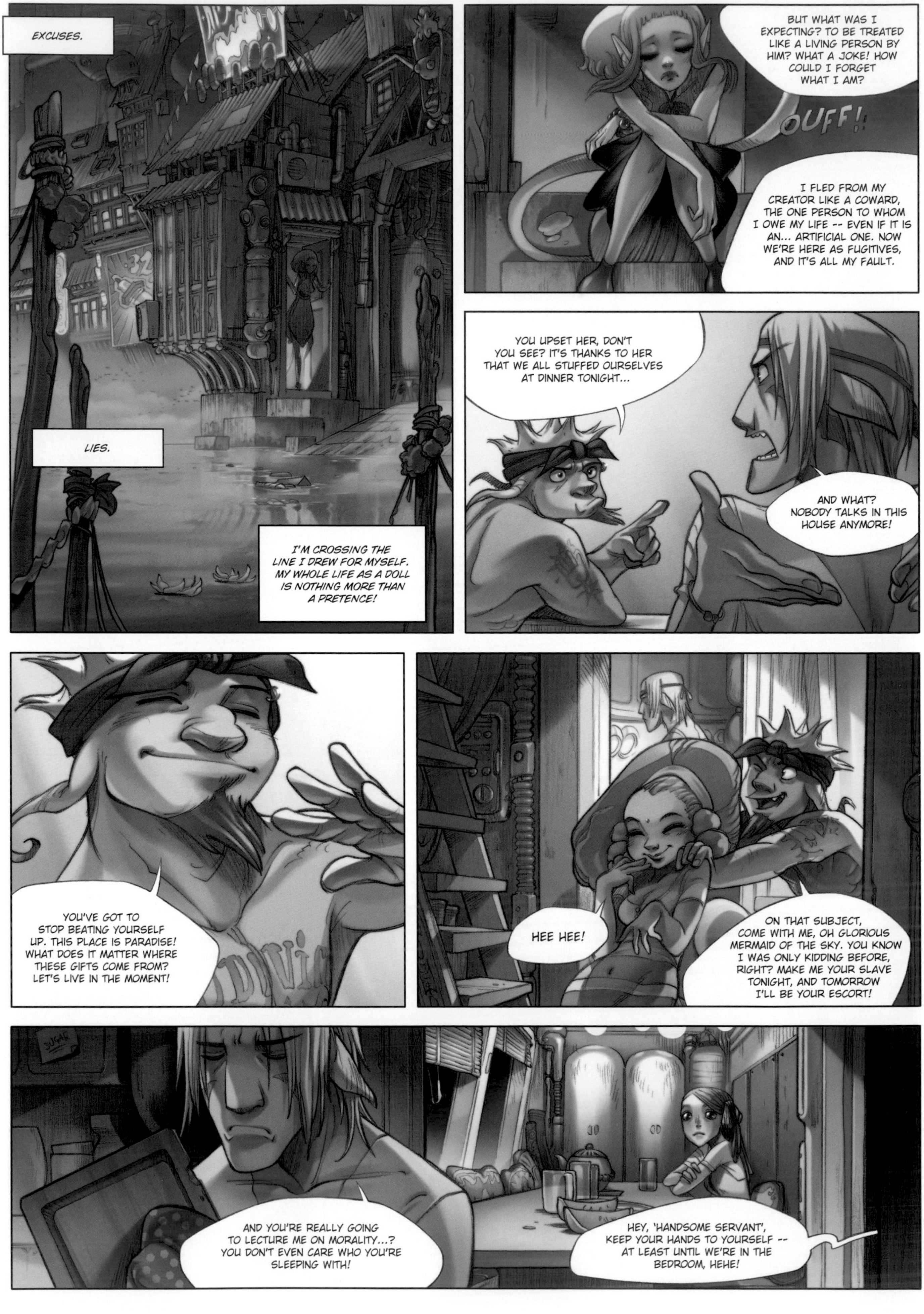
EXCUSES.
LIES.
I'M CROSSING THE LINE I DREW FOR MYSELF. MY WHOLE LIFE AS A DOLL IS NOTHING MORE THAN A PRETENCE!
BUT WHAT WAS I EXPECTING? TO BE TREATED LIKE A LIVING PERSON BY HIM? WHAT A JOKE! HOW COULD I FORGET WHAT I AM?
OUFF!!
I FLED FROM MY CREATOR LIKE A COWARD, THE ONE PERSON TO WHOM I OWE MY LIFE -- EVEN IF IT IS AN... ARTIFICIAL ONE. NOW WE'RE HERE AS FUGITIVES, AND IT'S ALL MY FAULT.
YOU UPSET HER, DON'T YOU SEE? IT'S THANKS TO HER THAT WE ALL STUFFED OURSELVES AT DINNER TONIGHT...
AND WHAT? NOBODY TALKS IN THIS HOUSE ANYMORE!
YOU'VE GOT TO STOP BEATING YOURSELF UP. THIS PLACE IS PARADISE! WHAT DOES IT MATTER WHERE THESE GIFTS COME FROM? LET'S LIVE IN THE MOMENT!
HEE HEE!
ON THAT SUBJECT, COME WITH ME, OH GLORIOUS MERMAID OF THE SKY. YOU KNOW I WAS ONLY KIDDING BEFORE, RIGHT? MAKE ME YOUR SLAVE TONIGHT, AND TOMORROW I'LL BE YOUR ESCORT!
SUGAR
AND YOU'RE REALLY GOING TO LECTURE ME ON MORALITY...? YOU DON'T EVEN CARE WHO YOU'RE SLEEPING WITH!
HEY, 'HANDSOME SERVANT', KEEP YOUR HANDS TO YOURSELF -- AT LEAST UNTIL WE'RE IN THE BEDROOM, HEHE!

MY DEAREST FAITHFUL ONES, WE ARE FINALLY ONLINE, HALLELUJAH!

HERE IS THE NEWS BULLETIN FOR THIS EVENING. LET US START WITH THE MOST UNPLEASANT ITEM: THE HEAD OF THE AGAPIEN MILITANTS IS STILL AT LARGE. THIS MERCILESS TRAITOR, KNOWN AS THE 'DOLL MAKER', IS MORE READILY KNOWN AS THE EX-POLITICAL AIDE TO OUR GLORIOUS LUDOVICA.

BUT IT'S NOT ALL BAD NEWS, MY DARLING VIEWERS!

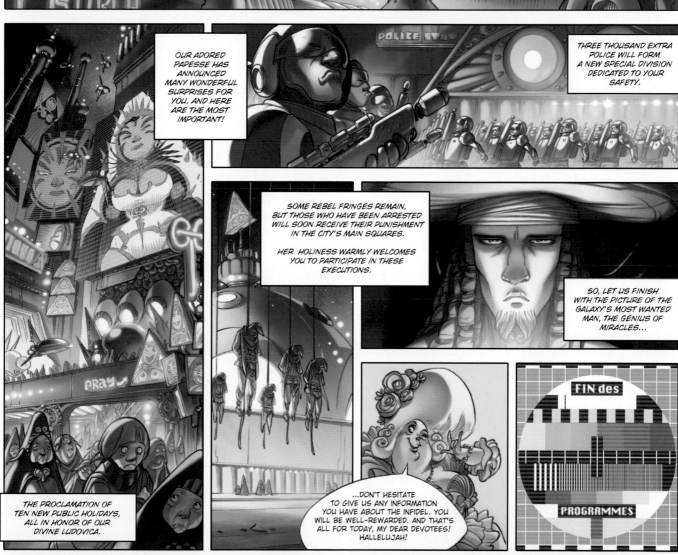

OUR ADORED PAPESSE HAS ANNOUNCED MANY WONDERFUL SURPRISES FOR YOU. AND HERE ARE THE MOST IMPORTANT!

THREE THOUSAND EXTRA POLICE WILL FORM A NEW SPECIAL DIVISION DEDICATED TO YOUR SAFETY.

SOME REBEL FRINGES REMAIN, BUT THOSE WHO HAVE BEEN ARRESTED WILL SOON RECEIVE THEIR PUNISHMENT IN THE CITY'S MAIN SQUARES.

HER HOLINESS WARMLY WELCOMES YOU TO PARTICIPATE IN THESE EXECUTIONS.

SO, LET US FINISH WITH THE PICTURE OF THE GALAXY'S MOST WANTED MAN, THE GENIUS OF MIRACLES...

THE PROCLAMATION OF TEN NEW PUBLIC HOLIDAYS, ALL IN HONOR OF OUR DIVINE LUDOVICA.

...DON'T HESITATE TO GIVE US ANY INFORMATION YOU HAVE ABOUT THE INFIDEL. YOU WILL BE WELL-REWARDED. AND THAT'S ALL FOR TODAY, MY DEAR DEVOTEES! HALLELUJAH!

FIN des

PROGRAMMES

LUDOVICA...

LUDOVICA...

WAKE UP,
MY SLEEPING BEAUTY!

OH, BUT LOOK AT YOU,
ACTING LIKE A LITTLE ORPHAN!
YOU SEEM A LITTLE LOST... YOU
SHOULD GET YOURSELF BACK IN
THE SADDLE, MY DEAR.

YOU!!

BLASTED TRAITOR!
HOW DARE YOU COME
BEFORE ME AFTER
EVERYTHING YOU'VE
DONE?

KRASH!

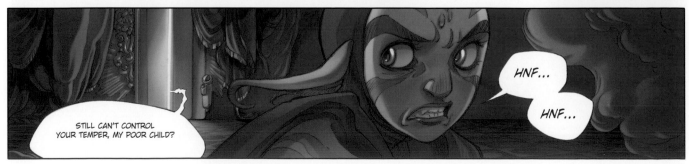

STILL CAN'T CONTROL
YOUR TEMPER, MY POOR CHILD?

HNF...

HNF...

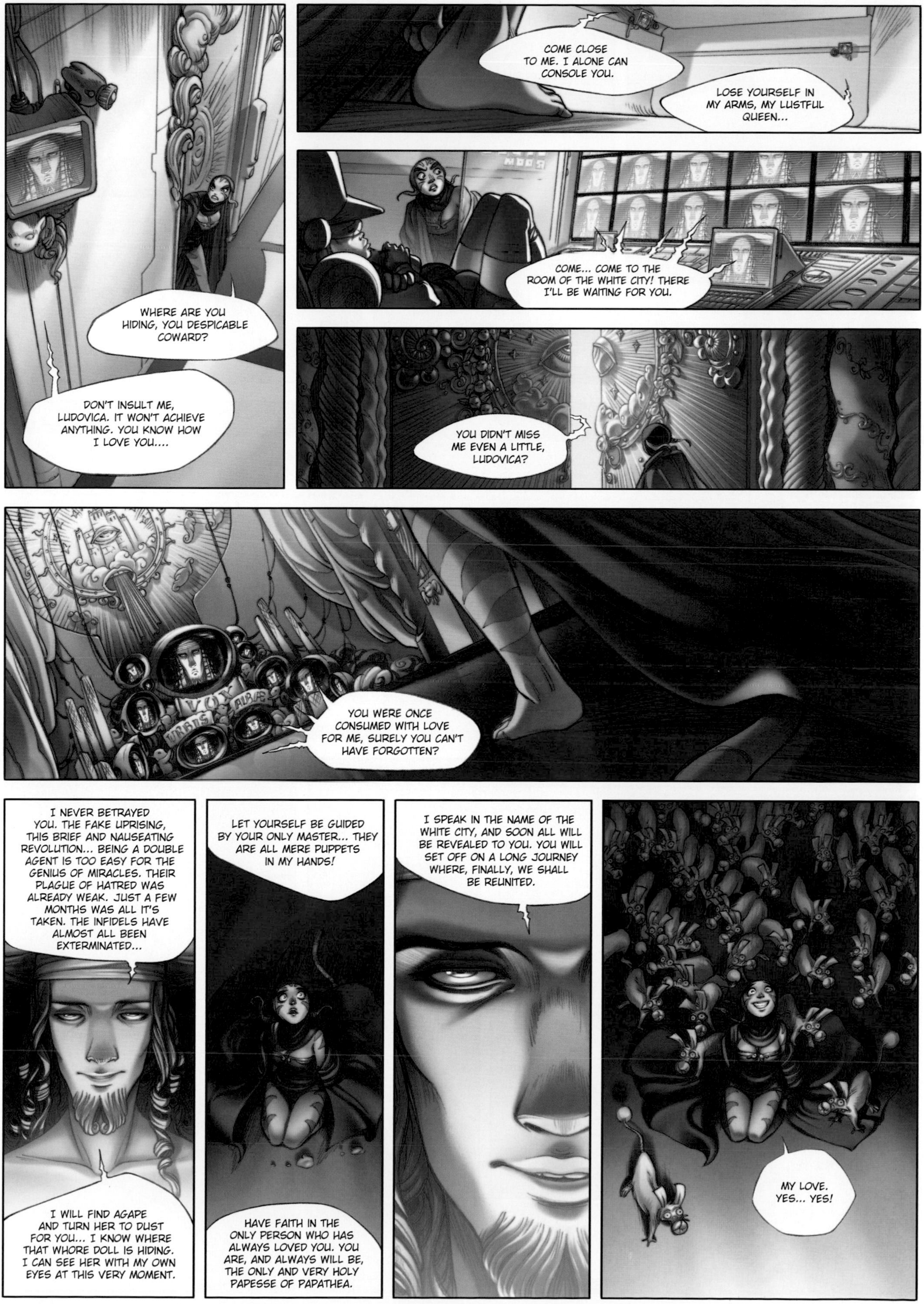
COME CLOSE TO ME. I ALONE CAN CONSOLE YOU.
LOSE YOURSELF IN MY ARMS, MY LUSTFUL QUEEN...
WHERE ARE YOU HIDING, YOU DESPICABLE COWARD?
DON'T INSULT ME, LUDOVICA. IT WON'T ACHIEVE ANYTHING. YOU KNOW HOW I LOVE YOU....
COME... COME TO THE ROOM OF THE WHITE CITY! THERE I'LL BE WAITING FOR YOU.
YOU DIDN'T MISS ME EVEN A LITTLE, LUDOVICA?
VOX URBIS ALBÆ
YOU WERE ONCE CONSUMED WITH LOVE FOR ME, SURELY YOU CAN'T HAVE FORGOTTEN?
I NEVER BETRAYED YOU. THE FAKE UPRISING, THIS BRIEF AND NAUSEATING REVOLUTION... BEING A DOUBLE AGENT IS TOO EASY FOR THE GENIUS OF MIRACLES. THEIR PLAGUE OF HATRED WAS ALREADY WEAK. JUST A FEW MONTHS WAS ALL IT'S TAKEN. THE INFIDELS HAVE ALMOST ALL BEEN EXTERMINATED...
I WILL FIND AGAPE AND TURN HER TO DUST FOR YOU... I KNOW WHERE THAT WHORE DOLL IS HIDING. I CAN SEE HER WITH MY OWN EYES AT THIS VERY MOMENT.
LET YOURSELF BE GUIDED BY YOUR ONLY MASTER... THEY ARE ALL MERE PUPPETS IN MY HANDS!
HAVE FAITH IN THE ONLY PERSON WHO HAS ALWAYS LOVED YOU. YOU ARE, AND ALWAYS WILL BE, THE ONLY AND VERY HOLY PAPESSE OF PAPATHEA.
I SPEAK IN THE NAME OF THE WHITE CITY, AND SOON ALL WILL BE REVEALED TO YOU. YOU WILL SET OFF ON A LONG JOURNEY WHERE, FINALLY, WE SHALL BE REUNITED.
MY LOVE. YES... YES!

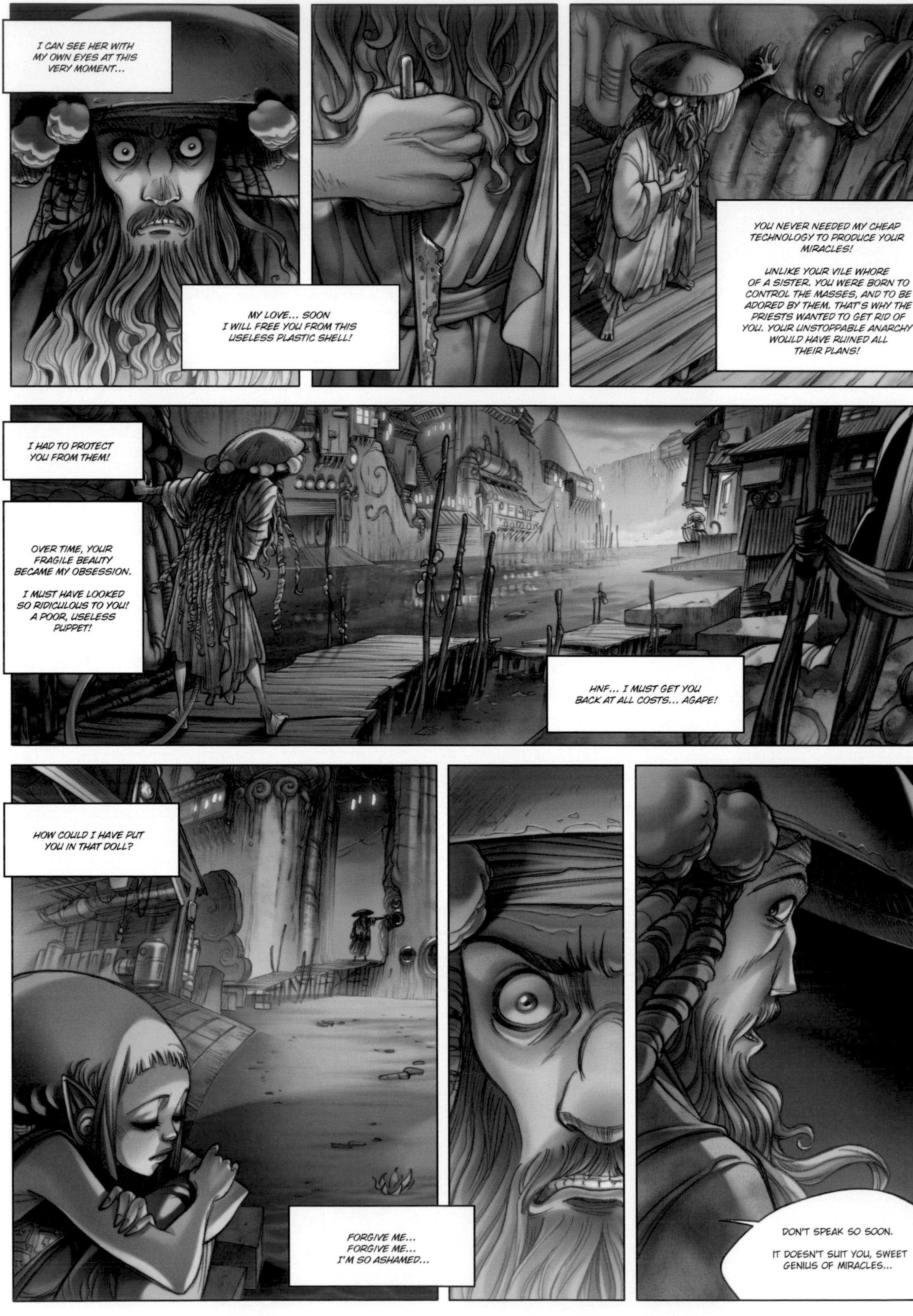
I CAN SEE HER WITH MY OWN EYES AT THIS VERY MOMENT...
MY LOVE... SOON I WILL FREE YOU FROM THIS USELESS PLASTIC SHELL!
YOU NEVER NEEDED MY CHEAP TECHNOLOGY TO PRODUCE YOUR MIRACLES!
UNLIKE YOUR VILE WHORE OF A SISTER. YOU WERE BORN TO CONTROL THE MASSES, AND TO BE ADORED BY THEM. THAT'S WHY THE PRIESTS WANTED TO GET RID OF YOU. YOUR UNSTOPPABLE ANARCHY WOULD HAVE RUINED ALL THEIR PLANS!
I HAD TO PROTECT YOU FROM THEM!
OVER TIME, YOUR FRAGILE BEAUTY BECAME MY OBSESSION.
I MUST HAVE LOOKED SO RIDICULOUS TO YOU! A POOR, USELESS PUPPET!
HNF... I MUST GET YOU BACK AT ALL COSTS... AGAPE!
HOW COULD I HAVE PUT YOU IN THAT DOLL?
FORGIVE ME... FORGIVE ME... I'M SO ASHAMED...
DON'T SPEAK SO SOON.
IT DOESN'T SUIT YOU, SWEET GENIUS OF MIRACLES...

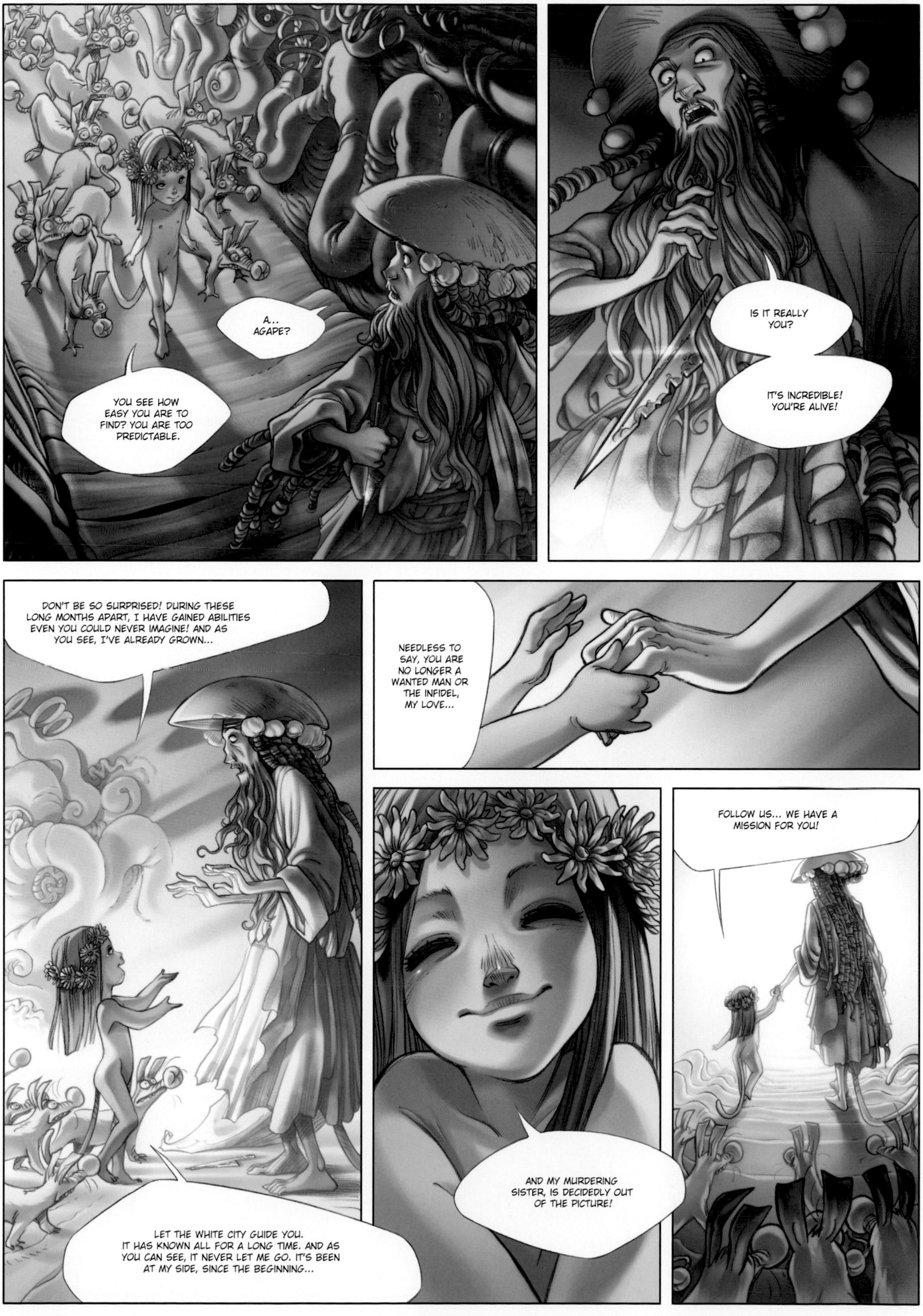
A... AGAPE?
YOU SEE HOW EASY YOU ARE TO FIND? YOU ARE TOO PREDICTABLE.
IS IT REALLY YOU?
IT'S INCREDIBLE! YOU'RE ALIVE!
DON'T BE SO SURPRISED! DURING THESE LONG MONTHS APART, I HAVE GAINED ABILITIES EVEN YOU COULD NEVER IMAGINE! AND AS YOU SEE, I'VE ALREADY GROWN...
LET THE WHITE CITY GUIDE YOU. IT HAS KNOWN ALL FOR A LONG TIME. AND AS YOU CAN SEE, IT NEVER LET ME GO. IT'S BEEN AT MY SIDE, SINCE THE BEGINNING...
NEEDLESS TO SAY, YOU ARE NO LONGER A WANTED MAN OR THE INFIDEL, MY LOVE...
AND MY MURDERING SISTER, IS DECIDEDLY OUT OF THE PICTURE!
FOLLOW US... WE HAVE A MISSION FOR YOU!

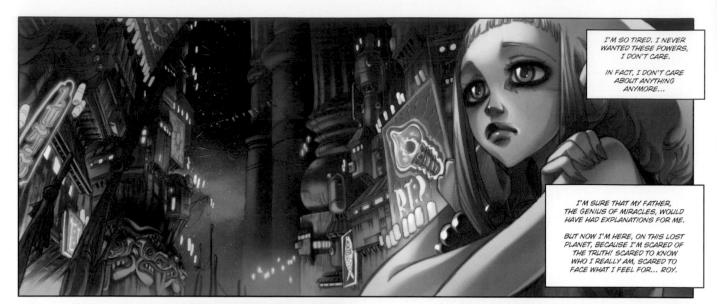

I'M SO TIRED. I NEVER WANTED THESE POWERS, I DON'T CARE.

IN FACT, I DON'T CARE ABOUT ANYTHING ANYMORE...

I'M SURE THAT MY FATHER, THE GENIUS OF MIRACLES, WOULD HAVE HAD EXPLANATIONS FOR ME.

BUT NOW I'M HERE, ON THIS LOST PLANET, BECAUSE I'M SCARED OF THE TRUTH! SCARED TO KNOW WHO I REALLY AM, SCARED TO FACE WHAT I FEEL FOR... ROY.

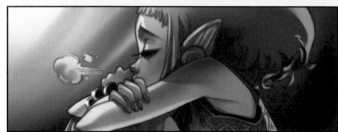

HM?

BUT...!

PLING!

WAIT...
I KNOW
YOU!

DLIN!

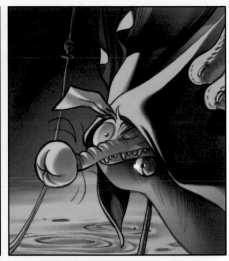

DLING!

DLING!

DLING!

ELIANTHE?

HOW...
HOW DID YOU
GET HERE?

DID SHE BRING
YOU?

BUT WHO
ARE YOU?!?

...AGAPE ?

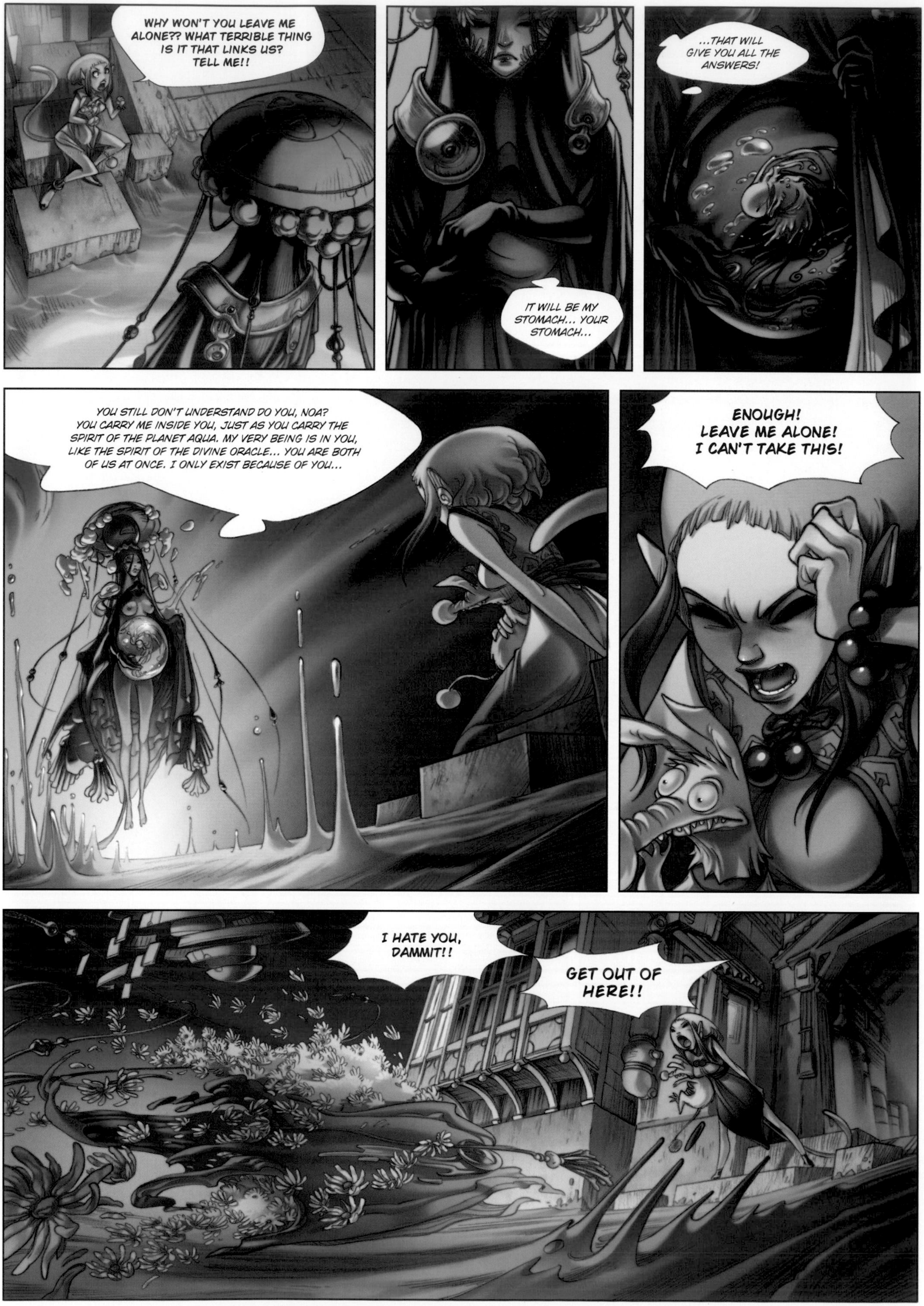
WHY WON'T YOU LEAVE ME ALONE?? WHAT TERRIBLE THING IS IT THAT LINKS US? TELL ME!!
IT WILL BE MY STOMACH... YOUR STOMACH...
...THAT WILL GIVE YOU ALL THE ANSWERS!
YOU STILL DON'T UNDERSTAND DO YOU, NOA? YOU CARRY ME INSIDE YOU, JUST AS YOU CARRY THE SPIRIT OF THE PLANET AQUA. MY VERY BEING IS IN YOU, LIKE THE SPIRIT OF THE DIVINE ORACLE... YOU ARE BOTH OF US AT ONCE. I ONLY EXIST BECAUSE OF YOU...
ENOUGH! LEAVE ME ALONE! I CAN'T TAKE THIS!
I HATE YOU, DAMMIT!!
GET OUT OF HERE!!

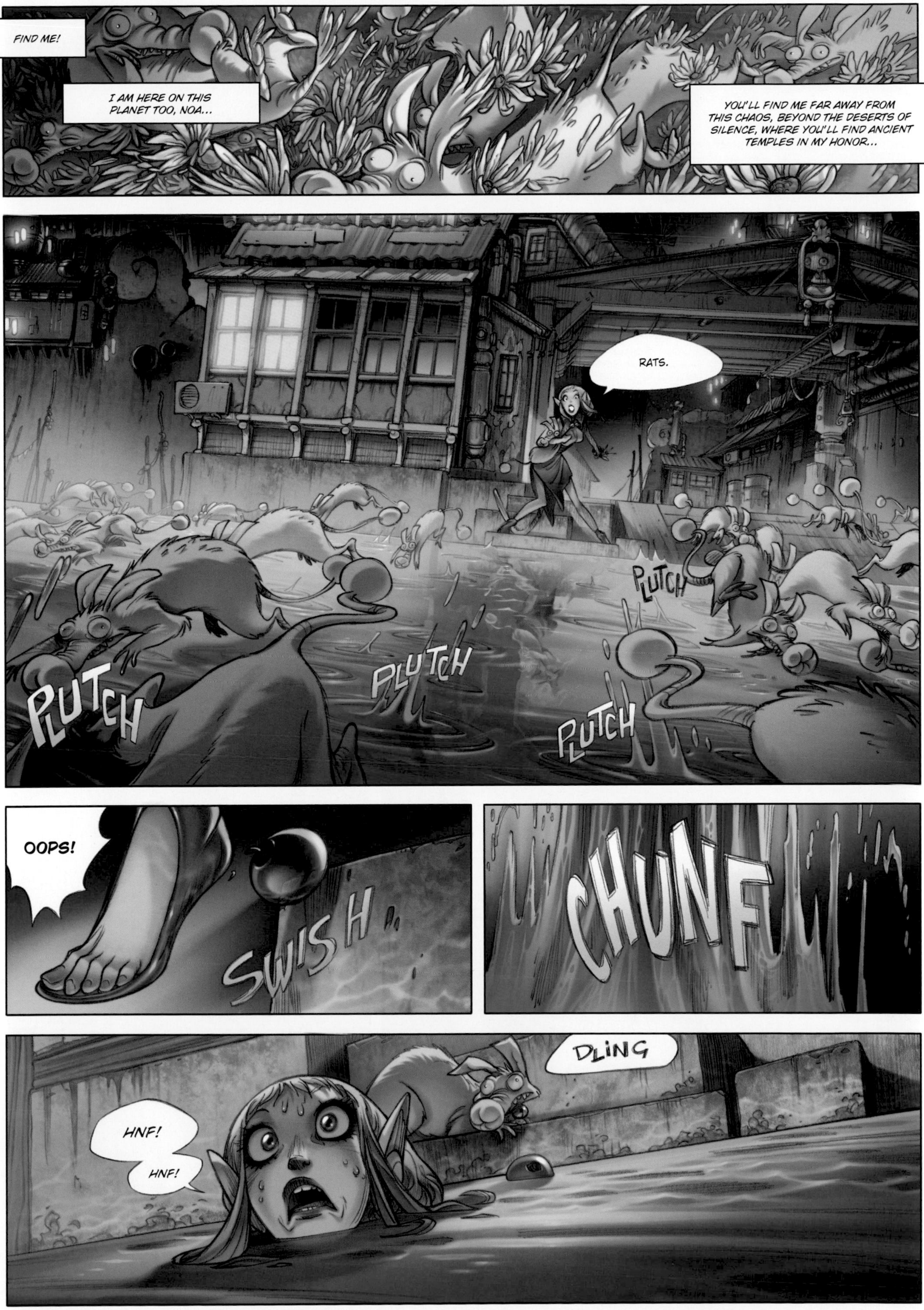
FIND ME!
I AM HERE ON THIS PLANET TOO, NOA...
YOU'LL FIND ME FAR AWAY FROM THIS CHAOS, BEYOND THE DESERTS OF SILENCE, WHERE YOU'LL FIND ANCIENT TEMPLES IN MY HONOR...
RATS.
PLUTCH
PLUTCH
PLUTCH
PLUTCH
OOPS!
SWISH
CHUNF
DLING
HNF!
HNF!

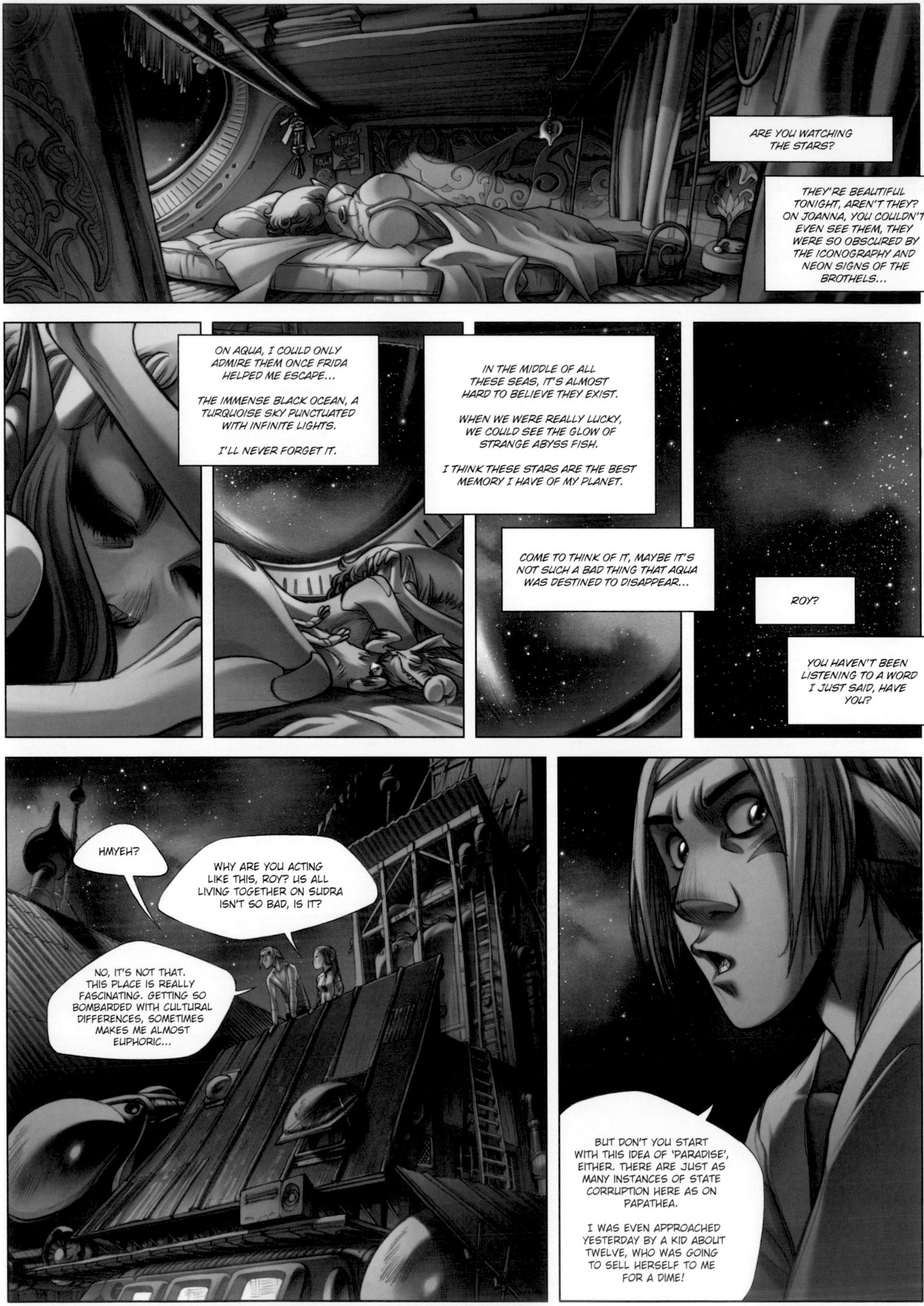
ARE YOU WATCHING THE STARS?
THEY'RE BEAUTIFUL TONIGHT, AREN'T THEY? ON JOANNA, YOU COULDN'T EVEN SEE THEM, THEY WERE SO OBSCURED BY THE ICONOGRAPHY AND NEON SIGNS OF THE BROTHELS...
ON AQUA, I COULD ONLY ADMIRE THEM ONCE FRIDA HELPED ME ESCAPE...
THE IMMENSE BLACK OCEAN, A TURQUOISE SKY PUNCTUATED WITH INFINITE LIGHTS.
I'LL NEVER FORGET IT.
IN THE MIDDLE OF ALL THESE SEAS, IT'S ALMOST HARD TO BELIEVE THEY EXIST.
WHEN WE WERE REALLY LUCKY, WE COULD SEE THE GLOW OF STRANGE ABYSS FISH.
I THINK THESE STARS ARE THE BEST MEMORY I HAVE OF MY PLANET.
COME TO THINK OF IT, MAYBE IT'S NOT SUCH A BAD THING THAT AQUA WAS DESTINED TO DISAPPEAR...
ROY?
YOU HAVEN'T BEEN LISTENING TO A WORD I JUST SAID, HAVE YOU?
HMYEH?
WHY ARE YOU ACTING LIKE THIS, ROY? US ALL LIVING TOGETHER ON SUDRA ISN'T SO BAD, IS IT?
NO, IT'S NOT THAT. THIS PLACE IS REALLY FASCINATING. GETTING SO BOMBARDED WITH CULTURAL DIFFERENCES, SOMETIMES MAKES ME ALMOST EUPHORIC...
BUT DON'T YOU START WITH THIS IDEA OF 'PARADISE', EITHER. THERE ARE JUST AS MANY INSTANCES OF STATE CORRUPTION HERE AS ON PAPATHEA.
I WAS EVEN APPROACHED YESTERDAY BY A KID ABOUT TWELVE, WHO WAS GOING TO SELL HERSELF TO ME FOR A DIME!

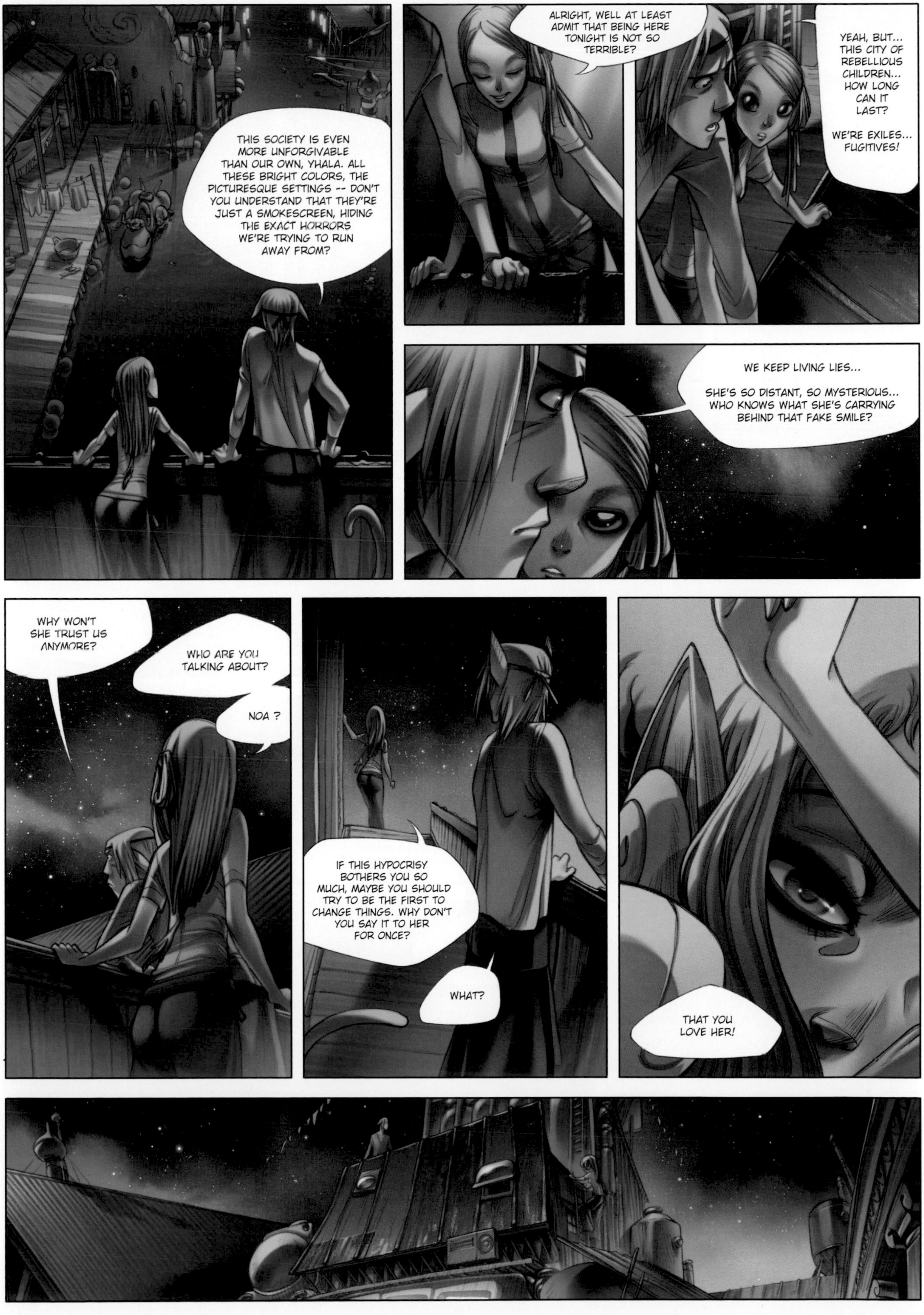

THIS SOCIETY IS EVEN MORE UNFORGIVABLE THAN OUR OWN, YHALA. ALL THESE BRIGHT COLORS, THE PICTURESQUE SETTINGS -- DON'T YOU UNDERSTAND THAT THEY'RE JUST A SMOKESCREEN, HIDING THE EXACT HORRORS WE'RE TRYING TO RUN AWAY FROM?
ALRIGHT, WELL AT LEAST ADMIT THAT BEING HERE TONIGHT IS NOT SO TERRIBLE?
YEAH, BUT... THIS CITY OF REBELLIOUS CHILDREN... HOW LONG CAN IT LAST?
WE'RE EXILES... FUGITIVES!
WE KEEP LIVING LIES...
SHE'S SO DISTANT, SO MYSTERIOUS... WHO KNOWS WHAT SHE'S CARRYING BEHIND THAT FAKE SMILE?
WHY WON'T SHE TRUST US ANYMORE?
WHO ARE YOU TALKING ABOUT?
NOA ?
IF THIS HYPOCRISY BOTHERS YOU SO MUCH, MAYBE YOU SHOULD TRY TO BE THE FIRST TO CHANGE THINGS. WHY DON'T YOU SAY IT TO HER FOR ONCE?
WHAT?
THAT YOU LOVE HER!

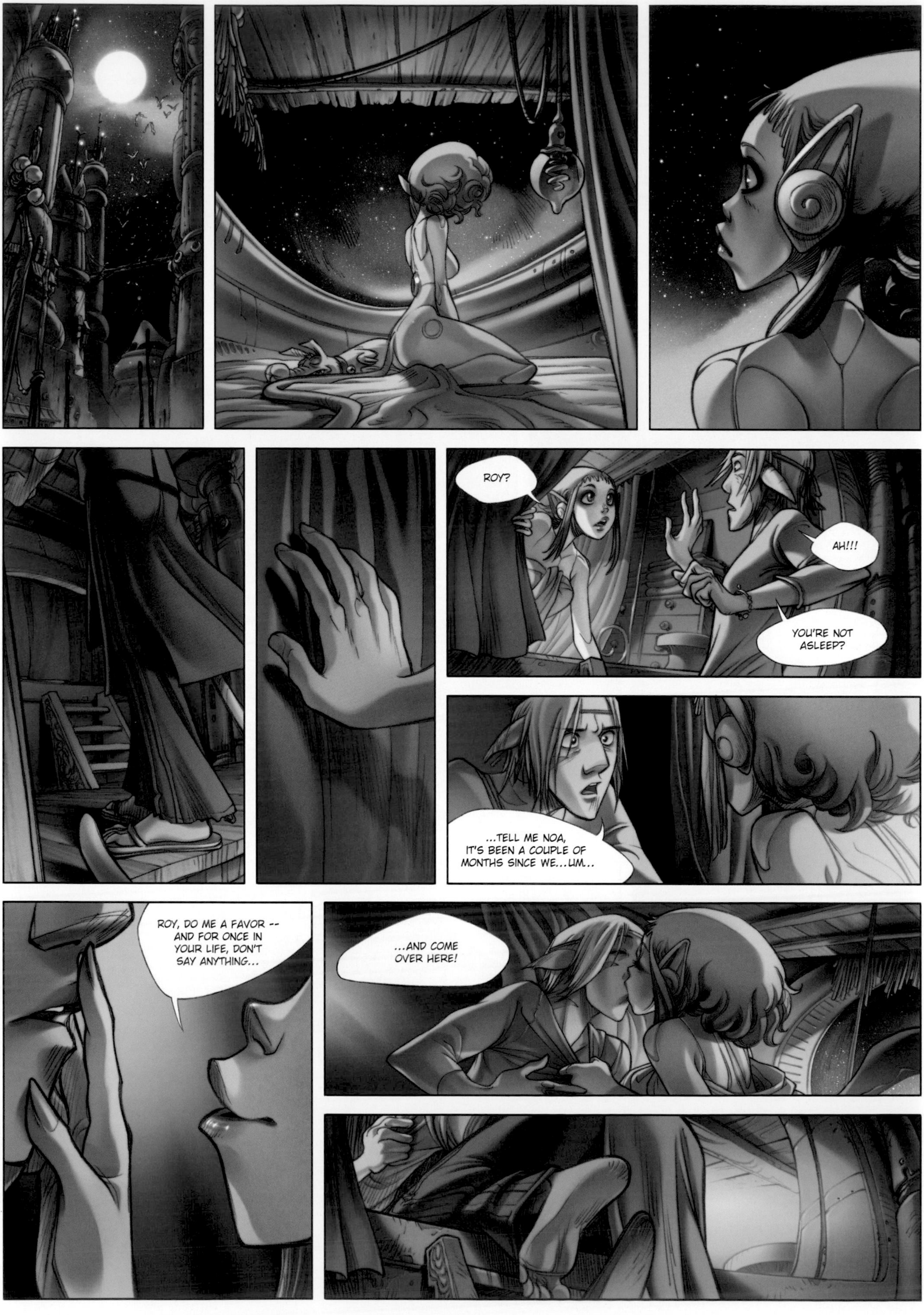
ROY?
AH!!!
YOU'RE NOT ASLEEP?
...TELL ME NOA, IT'S BEEN A COUPLE OF MONTHS SINCE WE...UM...
ROY, DO ME A FAVOR -- AND FOR ONCE IN YOUR LIFE, DON'T SAY ANYTHING...
...AND COME OVER HERE!

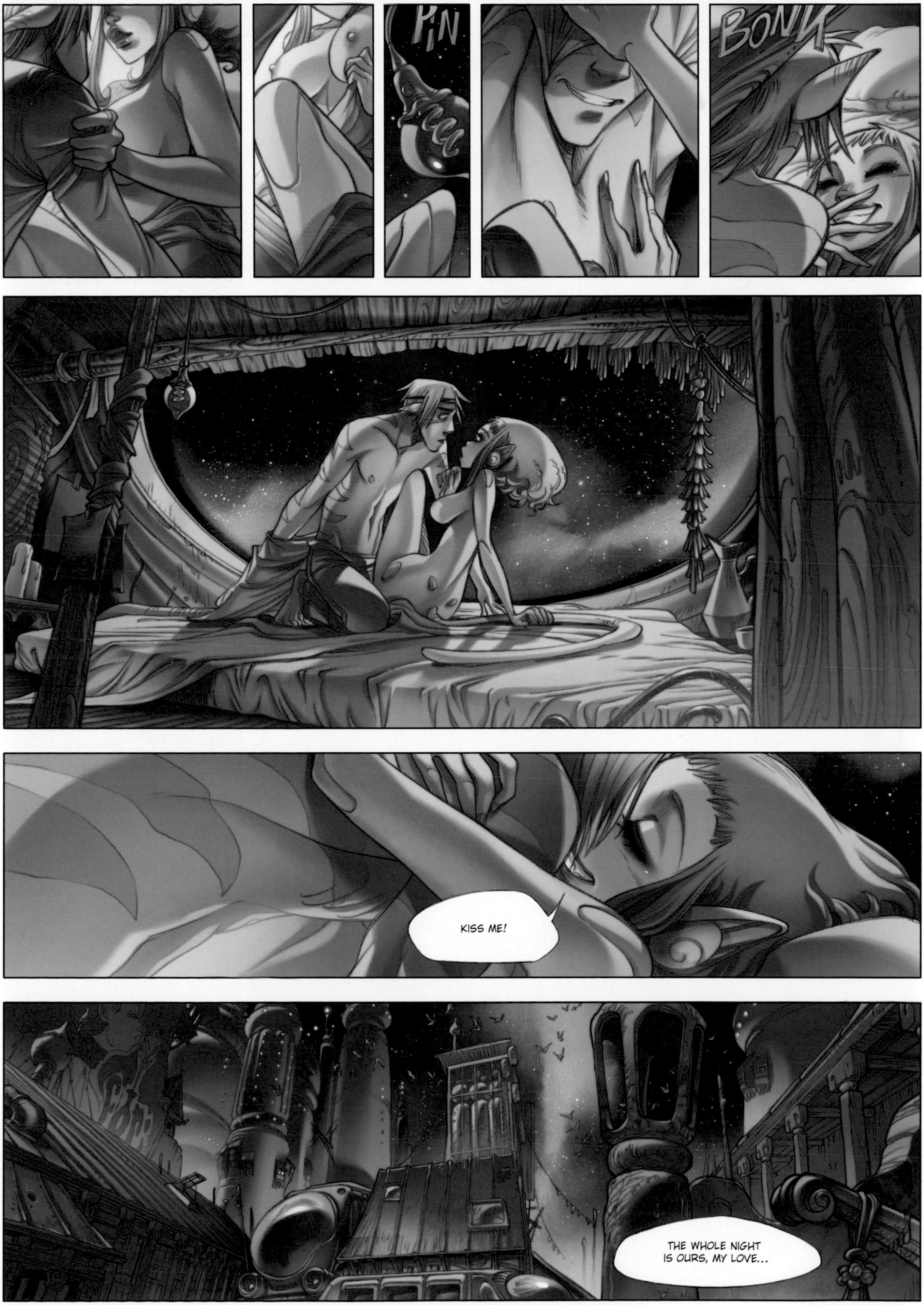
PIN
BONK
KISS ME!
THE WHOLE NIGHT IS OURS, MY LOVE...

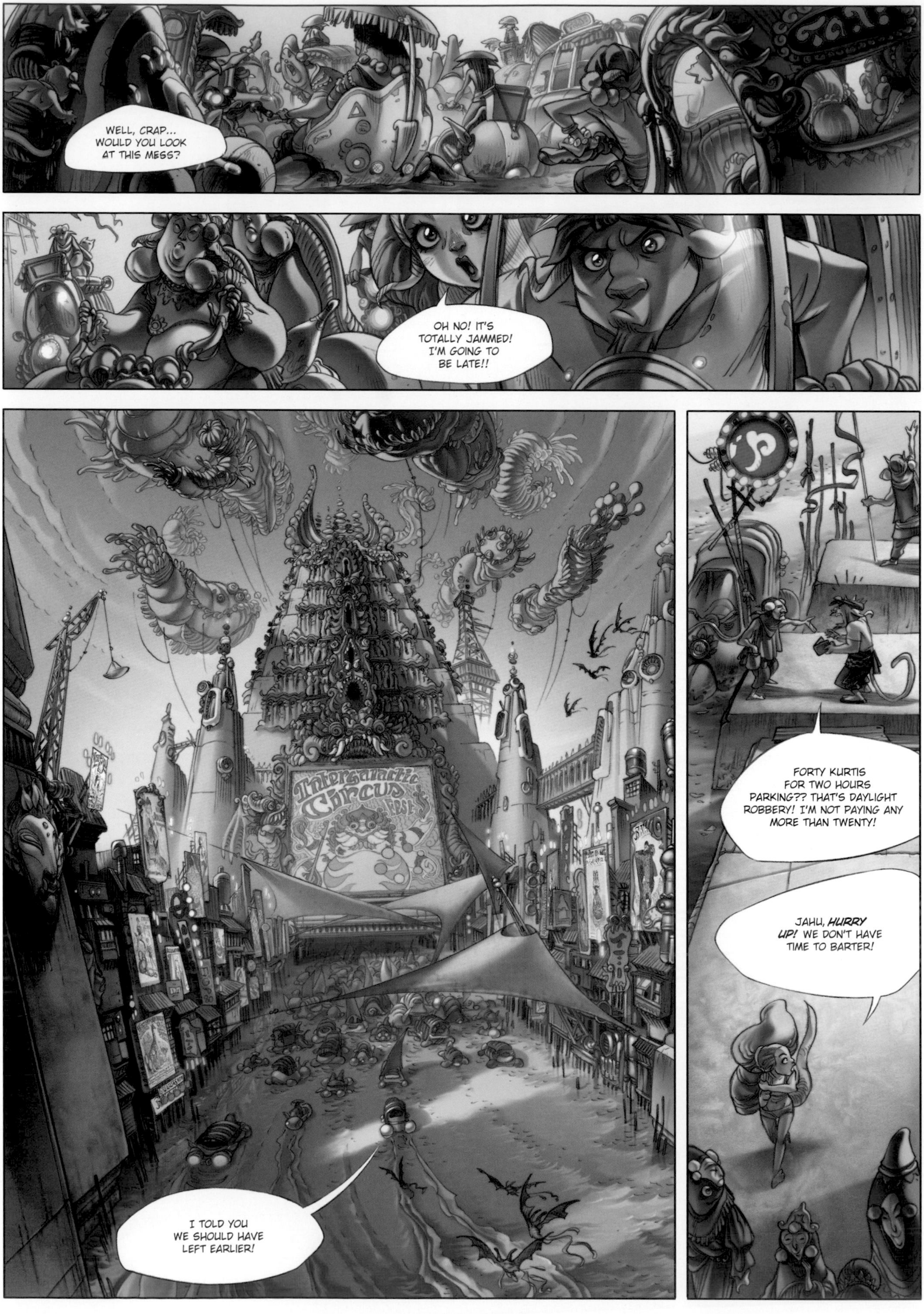
WELL, CRAP... WOULD YOU LOOK AT THIS MESS?
OH NO! IT'S TOTALLY JAMMED! I'M GOING TO BE LATE!!
I TOLD YOU WE SHOULD HAVE LEFT EARLIER!
FORTY KURTIS FOR TWO HOURS PARKING?? THAT'S DAYLIGHT ROBBERY! I'M NOT PAYING ANY MORE THAN TWENTY!
JAHU, *HURRY UP!* WE DON'T HAVE TIME TO BARTER!

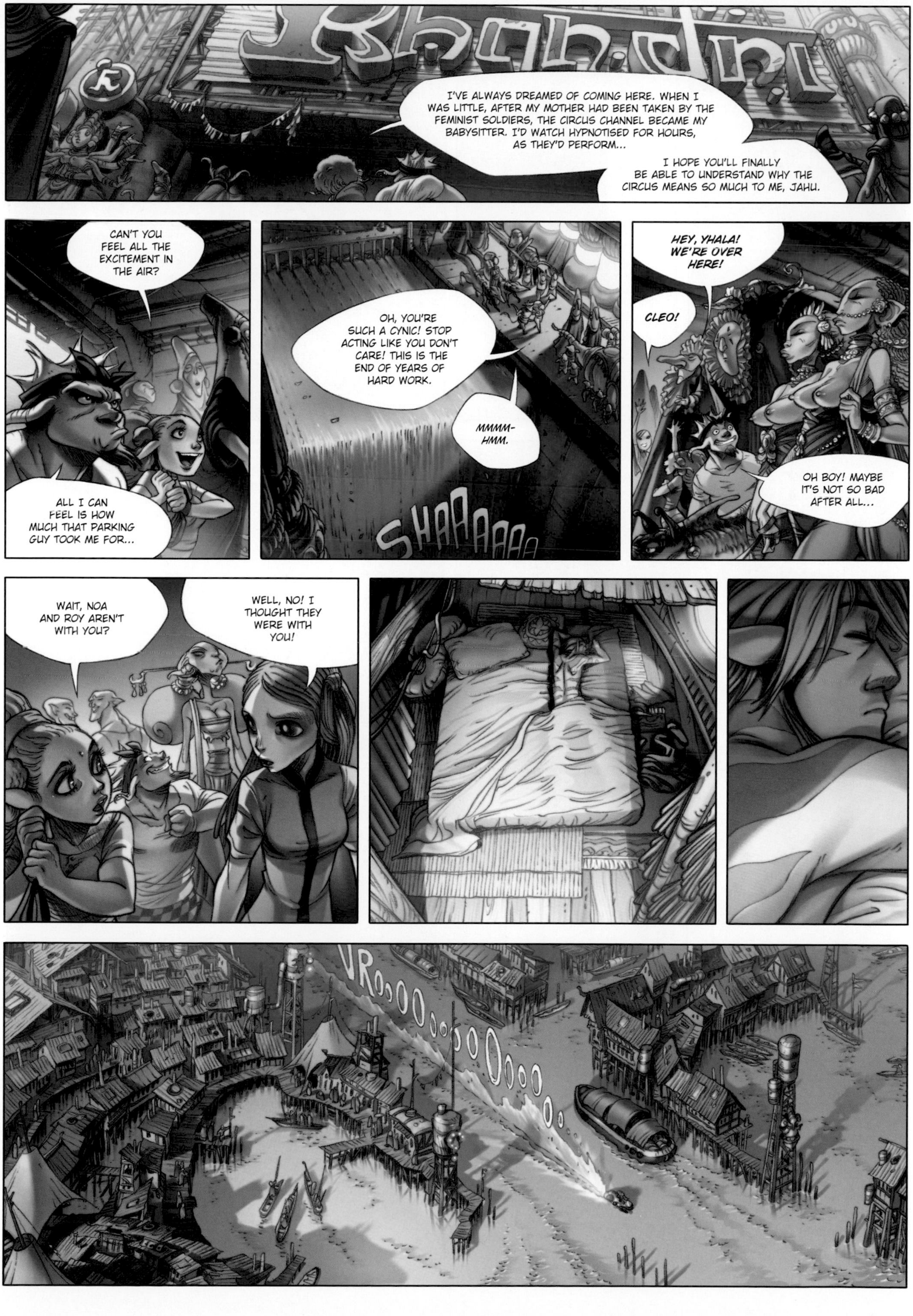
I'VE ALWAYS DREAMED OF COMING HERE. WHEN I WAS LITTLE, AFTER MY MOTHER HAD BEEN TAKEN BY THE FEMINIST SOLDIERS, THE CIRCUS CHANNEL BECAME MY BABYSITTER. I'D WATCH HYPNOTISED FOR HOURS, AS THEY'D PERFORM...
I HOPE YOU'LL FINALLY BE ABLE TO UNDERSTAND WHY THE CIRCUS MEANS SO MUCH TO ME, JAHU.
CAN'T YOU FEEL ALL THE EXCITEMENT IN THE AIR?
ALL I CAN FEEL IS HOW MUCH THAT PARKING GUY TOOK ME FOR...
OH, YOU'RE SUCH A CYNIC! STOP ACTING LIKE YOU DON'T CARE! THIS IS THE END OF YEARS OF HARD WORK.
MMMM-HMM.
SHAAAAAA
HEY, YHALA! WE'RE OVER HERE!
CLEO!
OH BOY! MAYBE IT'S NOT SO BAD AFTER ALL...
WAIT, NOA AND ROY AREN'T WITH YOU?
WELL, NO! I THOUGHT THEY WERE WITH YOU!
VROOOOOOOOOOOO

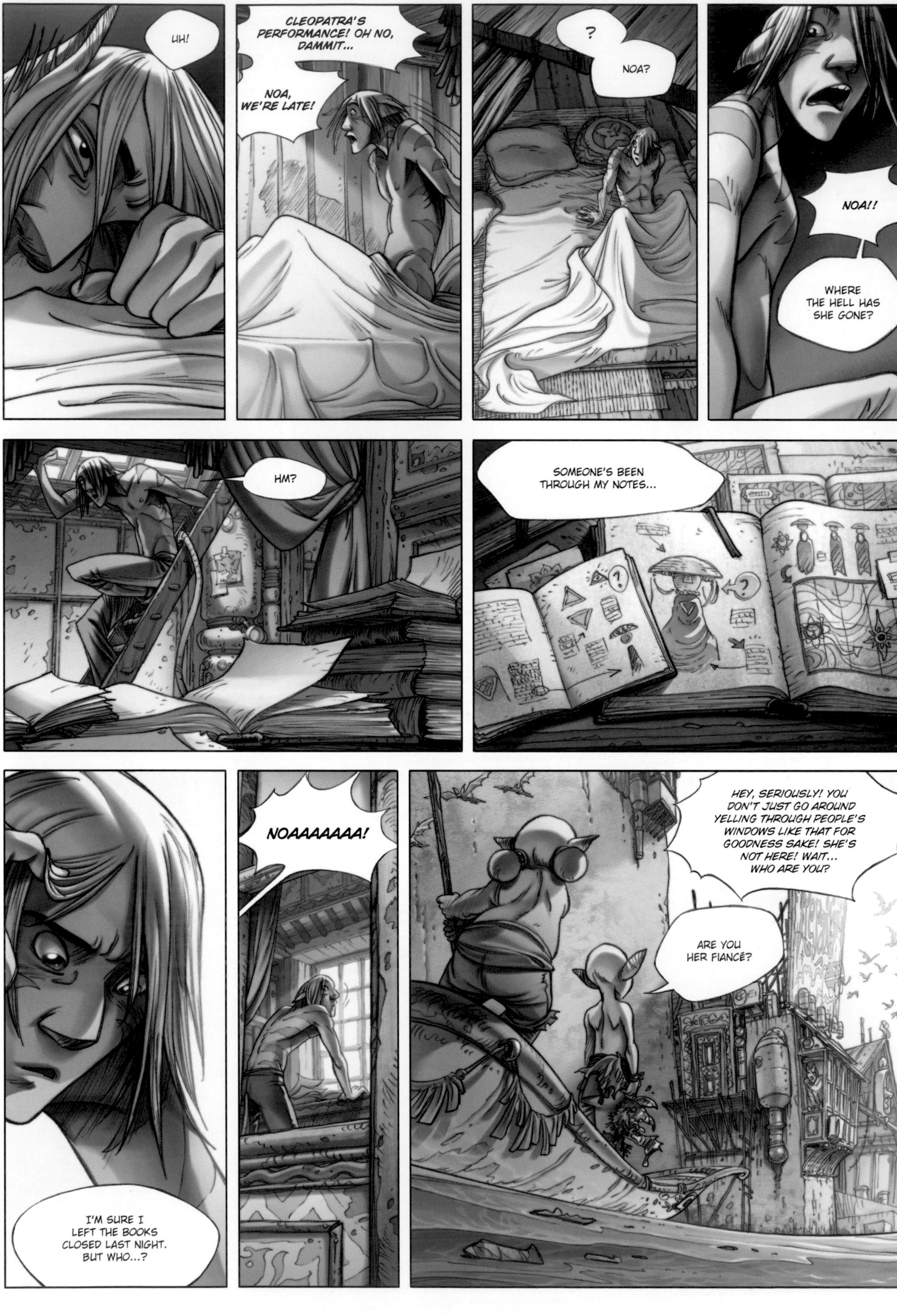
UH!
CLEOPATRA'S PERFORMANCE! OH NO, DAMMIT...
NOA, WE'RE LATE!
?
NOA?
NOA!!
WHERE THE HELL HAS SHE GONE?
HM?
SOMEONE'S BEEN THROUGH MY NOTES...
I'M SURE I LEFT THE BOOKS CLOSED LAST NIGHT. BUT WHO...?
NOAAAAAAA!
HEY, SERIOUSLY! YOU DON'T JUST GO AROUND YELLING THROUGH PEOPLE'S WINDOWS LIKE THAT FOR GOODNESS SAKE! SHE'S NOT HERE! WAIT... WHO ARE YOU?
ARE YOU HER FIANCÉ?

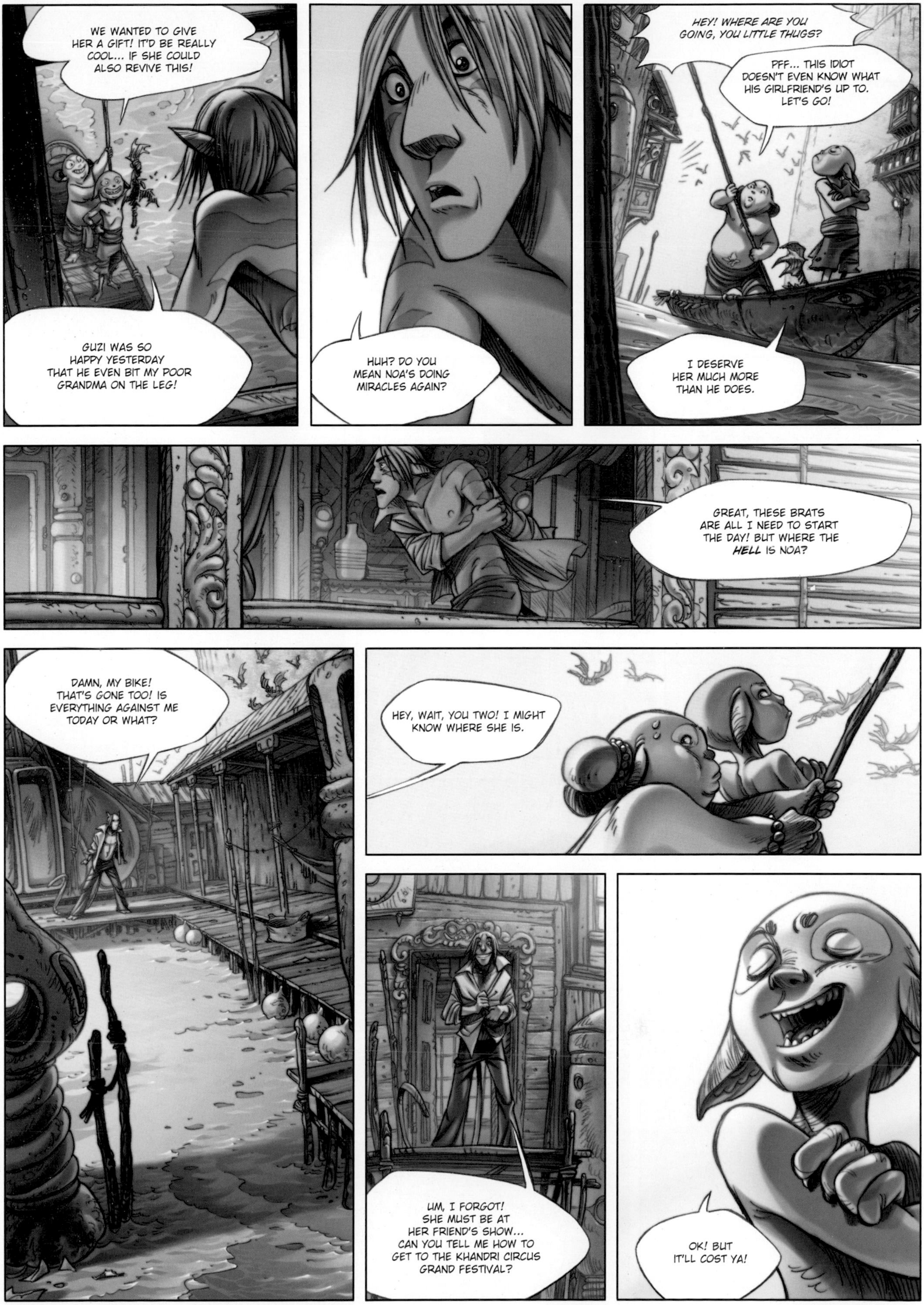
WE WANTED TO GIVE HER A GIFT! IT'D BE REALLY COOL... IF SHE COULD ALSO REVIVE THIS!
GUZI WAS SO HAPPY YESTERDAY THAT HE EVEN BIT MY POOR GRANDMA ON THE LEG!
HUH? DO YOU MEAN NOA'S DOING MIRACLES AGAIN?
HEY! WHERE ARE YOU GOING, YOU LITTLE THUGS?
PFF... THIS IDIOT DOESN'T EVEN KNOW WHAT HIS GIRLFRIEND'S UP TO. LET'S GO!
I DESERVE HER MUCH MORE THAN HE DOES.
GREAT, THESE BRATS ARE ALL I NEED TO START THE DAY! BUT WHERE THE HELL IS NOA?
DAMN, MY BIKE! THAT'S GONE TOO! IS EVERYTHING AGAINST ME TODAY OR WHAT?
HEY, WAIT, YOU TWO! I MIGHT KNOW WHERE SHE IS.
UM, I FORGOT! SHE MUST BE AT HER FRIEND'S SHOW... CAN YOU TELL ME HOW TO GET TO THE KHANDRI CIRCUS GRAND FESTIVAL?
OK! BUT IT'LL COST YA!

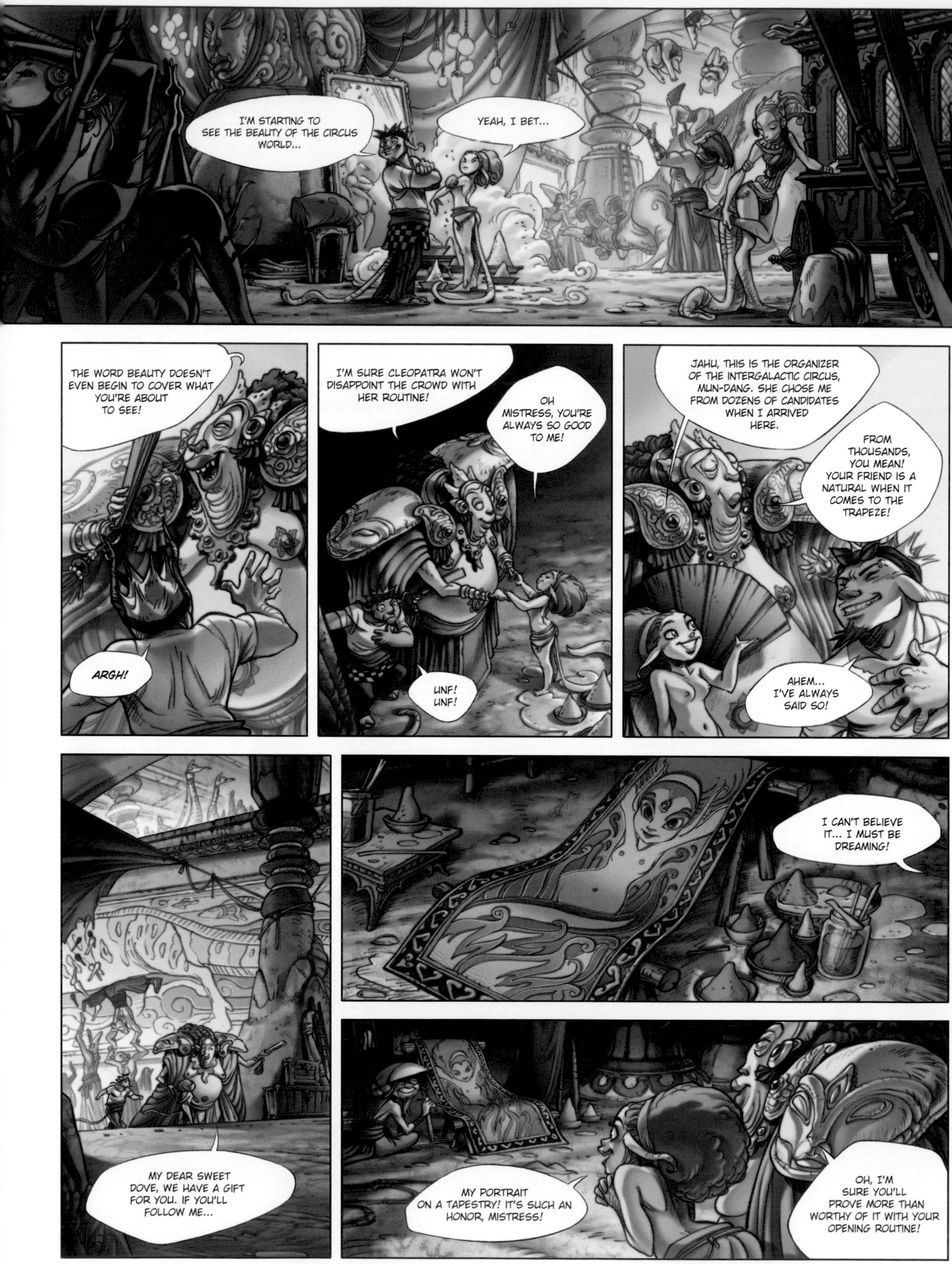

I'M STARTING TO SEE THE BEAUTY OF THE CIRCUS WORLD...
YEAH, I BET...
THE WORD BEAUTY DOESN'T EVEN BEGIN TO COVER WHAT YOU'RE ABOUT TO SEE!
ARGH!
I'M SURE CLEOPATRA WON'T DISAPPOINT THE CROWD WITH HER ROUTINE!
OH MISTRESS, YOU'RE ALWAYS SO GOOD TO ME!
UNF! UNF!
JAHU, THIS IS THE ORGANIZER OF THE INTERGALACTIC CIRCUS, MUN-DANG. SHE CHOSE ME FROM DOZENS OF CANDIDATES WHEN I ARRIVED HERE.
FROM THOUSANDS, YOU MEAN! YOUR FRIEND IS A NATURAL WHEN IT COMES TO THE TRAPEZE!
AHEM... I'VE ALWAYS SAID SO!
MY DEAR SWEET DOVE, WE HAVE A GIFT FOR YOU. IF YOU'LL FOLLOW ME...
I CAN'T BELIEVE IT... I MUST BE DREAMING!
MY PORTRAIT ON A TAPESTRY! IT'S SUCH AN HONOR, MISTRESS!
OH, I'M SURE YOU'LL PROVE MORE THAN WORTHY OF IT WITH YOUR OPENING ROUTINE!

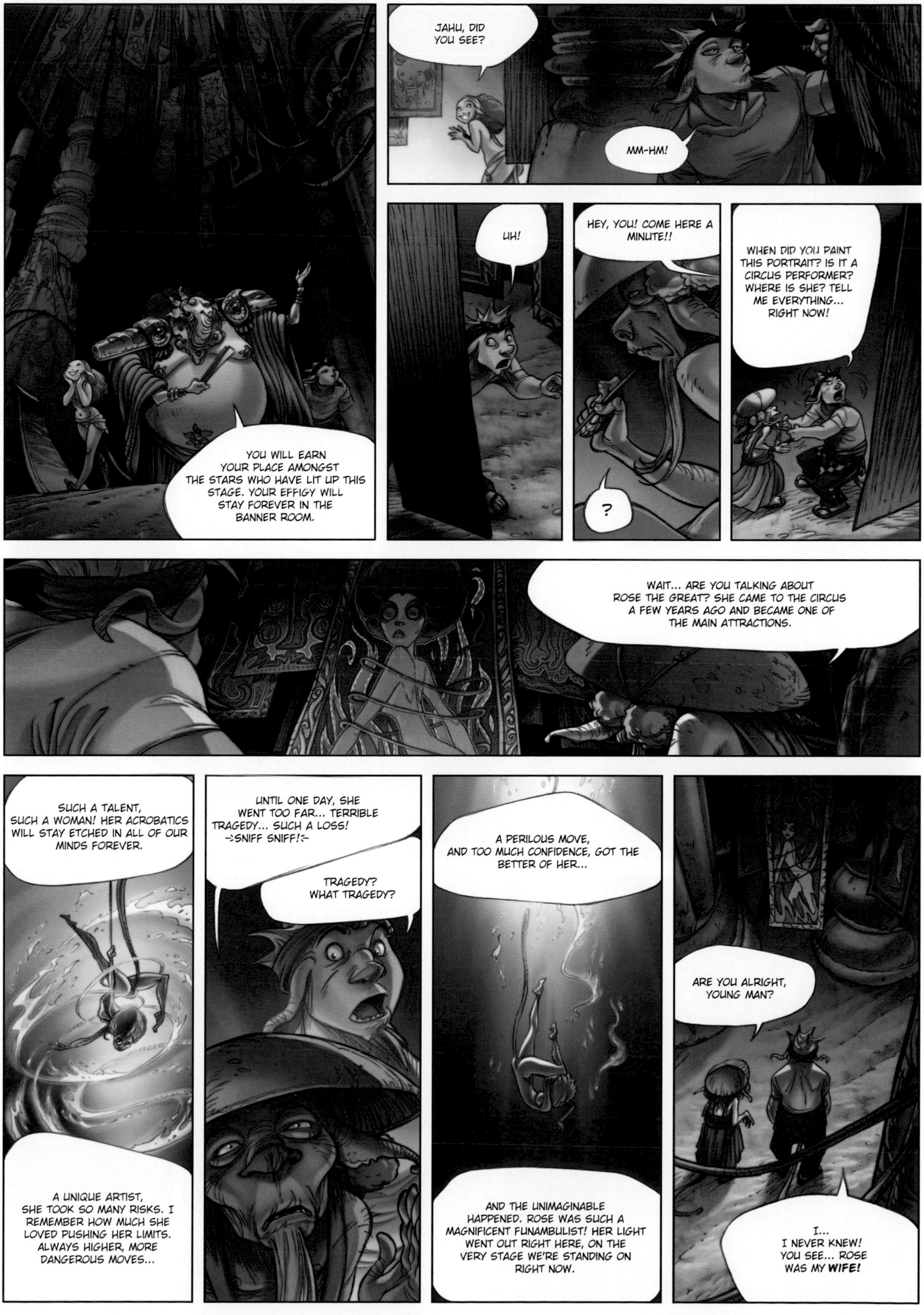
YOU WILL EARN YOUR PLACE AMONGST THE STARS WHO HAVE LIT UP THIS STAGE. YOUR EFFIGY WILL STAY FOREVER IN THE BANNER ROOM.
JAHU, DID YOU SEE?
MM-HM!
UH!
HEY, YOU! COME HERE A MINUTE!!
?
WHEN DID YOU PAINT THIS PORTRAIT? IS IT A CIRCUS PERFORMER? WHERE IS SHE? TELL ME EVERYTHING... RIGHT NOW!
WAIT... ARE YOU TALKING ABOUT ROSE THE GREAT? SHE CAME TO THE CIRCUS A FEW YEARS AGO AND BECAME ONE OF THE MAIN ATTRACTIONS.
SUCH A TALENT, SUCH A WOMAN! HER ACROBATICS WILL STAY ETCHED IN ALL OF OUR MINDS FOREVER.
A UNIQUE ARTIST, SHE TOOK SO MANY RISKS. I REMEMBER HOW MUCH SHE LOVED PUSHING HER LIMITS. ALWAYS HIGHER, MORE DANGEROUS MOVES...
UNTIL ONE DAY, SHE WENT TOO FAR... TERRIBLE TRAGEDY... SUCH A LOSS! ->SNIFF SNIFF!<-
TRAGEDY? WHAT TRAGEDY?
A PERILOUS MOVE, AND TOO MUCH CONFIDENCE, GOT THE BETTER OF HER...
AND THE UNIMAGINABLE HAPPENED. ROSE WAS SUCH A MAGNIFICENT FUNAMBULIST! HER LIGHT WENT OUT RIGHT HERE, ON THE VERY STAGE WE'RE STANDING ON RIGHT NOW.
ARE YOU ALRIGHT, YOUNG MAN?
I... I NEVER KNEW! YOU SEE... ROSE WAS MY **WIFE!**

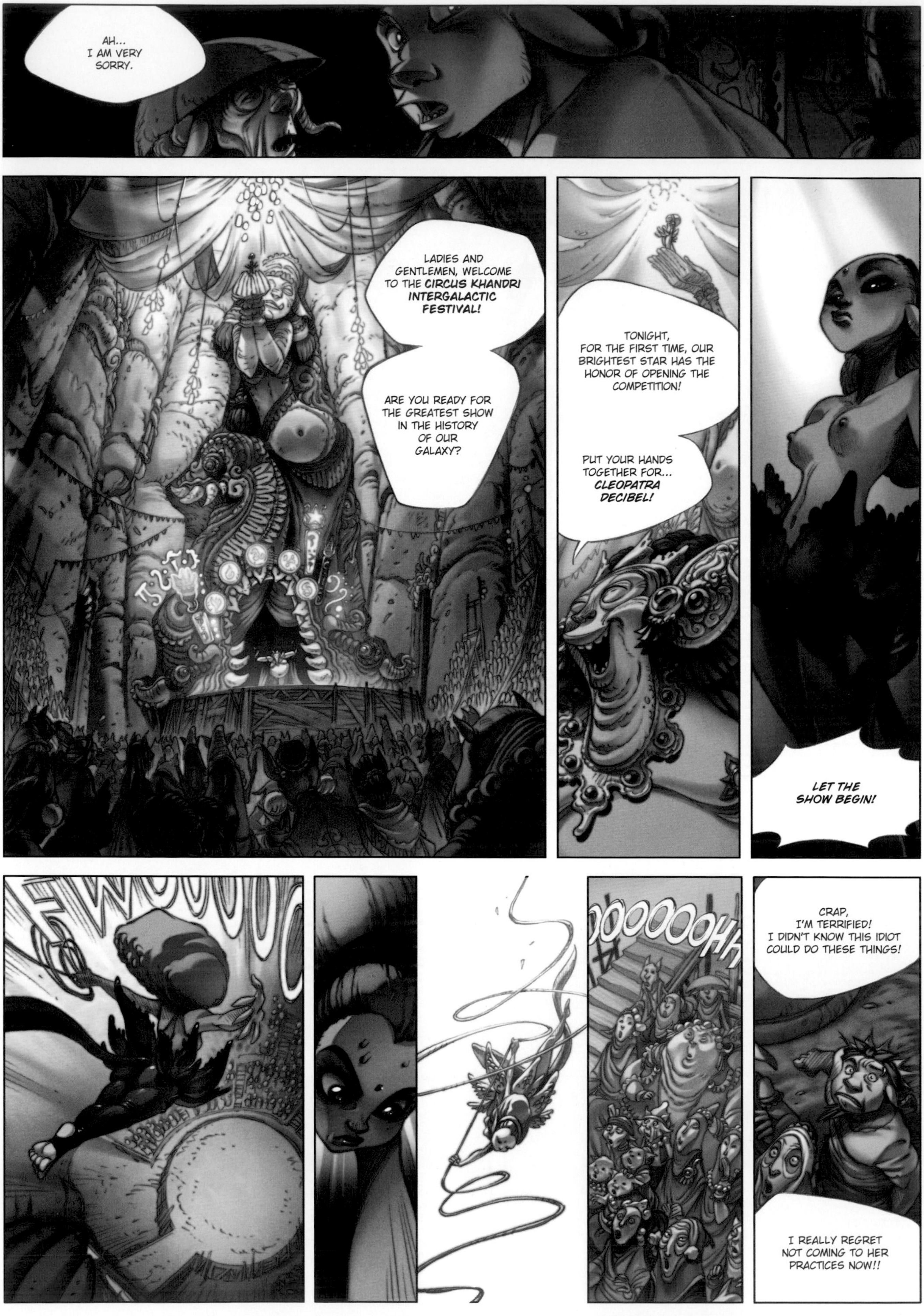
AH... I AM VERY SORRY.
LADIES AND GENTLEMEN, WELCOME TO THE **CIRCUS KHANDRI INTERGALACTIC FESTIVAL!**
ARE YOU READY FOR THE GREATEST SHOW IN THE HISTORY OF OUR GALAXY?
TONIGHT, FOR THE FIRST TIME, OUR BRIGHTEST STAR HAS THE HONOR OF OPENING THE COMPETITION!
PUT YOUR HANDS TOGETHER FOR... ***CLEOPATRA DECIBEL!***
LET THE SHOW BEGIN!
WOOOO
OOOOOOOHH
CRAP, I'M TERRIFIED! I DIDN'T KNOW THIS IDIOT COULD DO THESE THINGS!
I REALLY REGRET NOT COMING TO HER PRACTICES NOW!!

WE'RE THE BEST!

YEAH!

WE'RE GOING TO END UP WITH BROKEN BONES!

WE SAID WE KNEW THE FASTEST ROUTE, NOT THE EASIEST...

DON'T GIVE UP, OLD MAN! COME ON, WE'RE ALMOST THERE!

OLD MAN?

OK, NOA'S FIANCÉ! HERE'S YOUR CIRCUS!

TA DA!

-»HUFF...
HUFF...«-

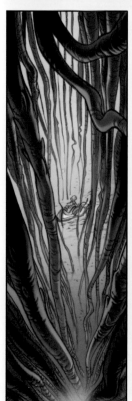

I HOPE I'M NOT LOST AGAIN, SIGH!

THE MAP DID POINT ME TO THIS PART OF THE RIVER...

STUPID VINES!! WE'LL NEVER GET OUT OF THIS RIVER FOREST ALIVE... THEY'RE EVERYWHERE!

HOLD ON, I THINK I SEE THE WAY OUT!

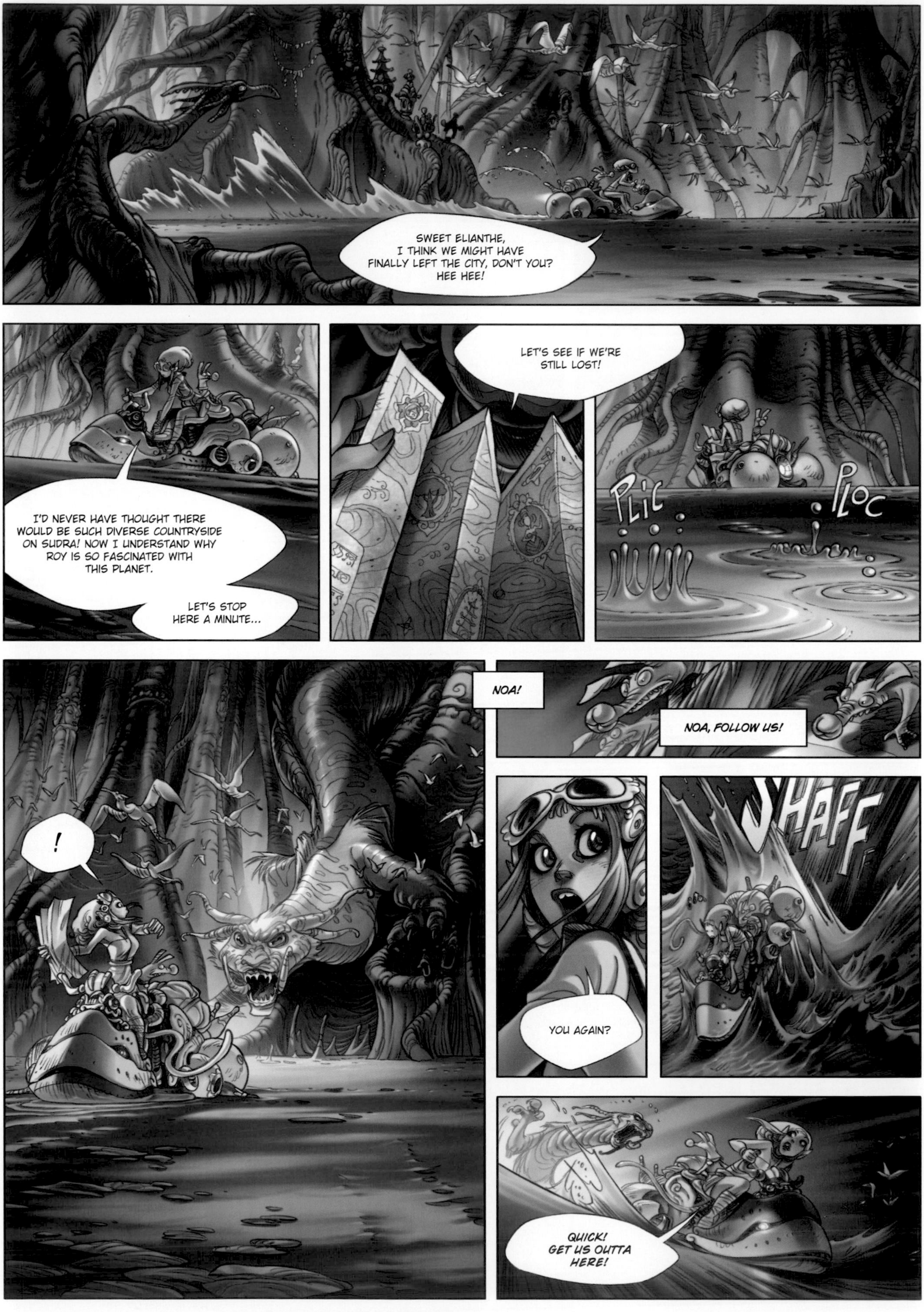
SWEET ELIANTHE, I THINK WE MIGHT HAVE FINALLY LEFT THE CITY, DON'T YOU? HEE HEE!
I'D NEVER HAVE THOUGHT THERE WOULD BE SUCH DIVERSE COUNTRYSIDE ON SUDRA! NOW I UNDERSTAND WHY ROY IS SO FASCINATED WITH THIS PLANET.
LET'S STOP HERE A MINUTE...
LET'S SEE IF WE'RE STILL LOST!
PLIC
PLOC
!
NOA!
NOA, FOLLOW US!
YOU AGAIN?
SHAFF
QUICK! GET US OUTTA HERE!

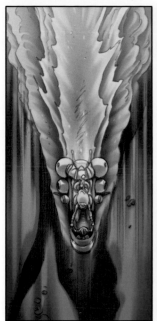

AAAH!

OOF! THOSE TEETH!

GET AWAY!!
I DON'T WANT
TO HAVE TO
KILL YOU!

HNF,
HNF!

RRRRRRR

THERE!

NOW YOU KNOW
WHO'S BOSS!

!

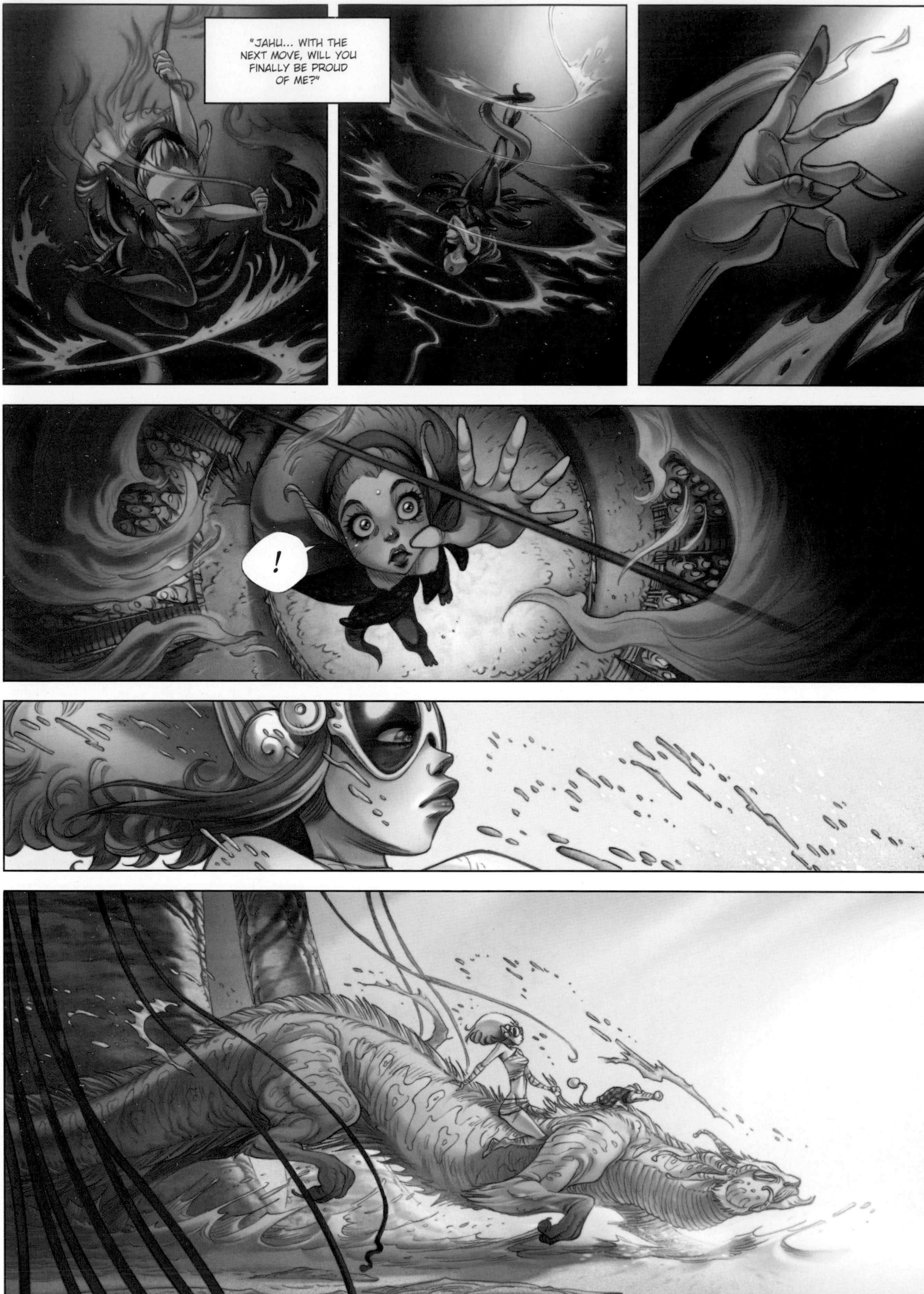
"JAHU... WITH THE NEXT MOVE, WILL YOU FINALLY BE PROUD OF ME?"
!

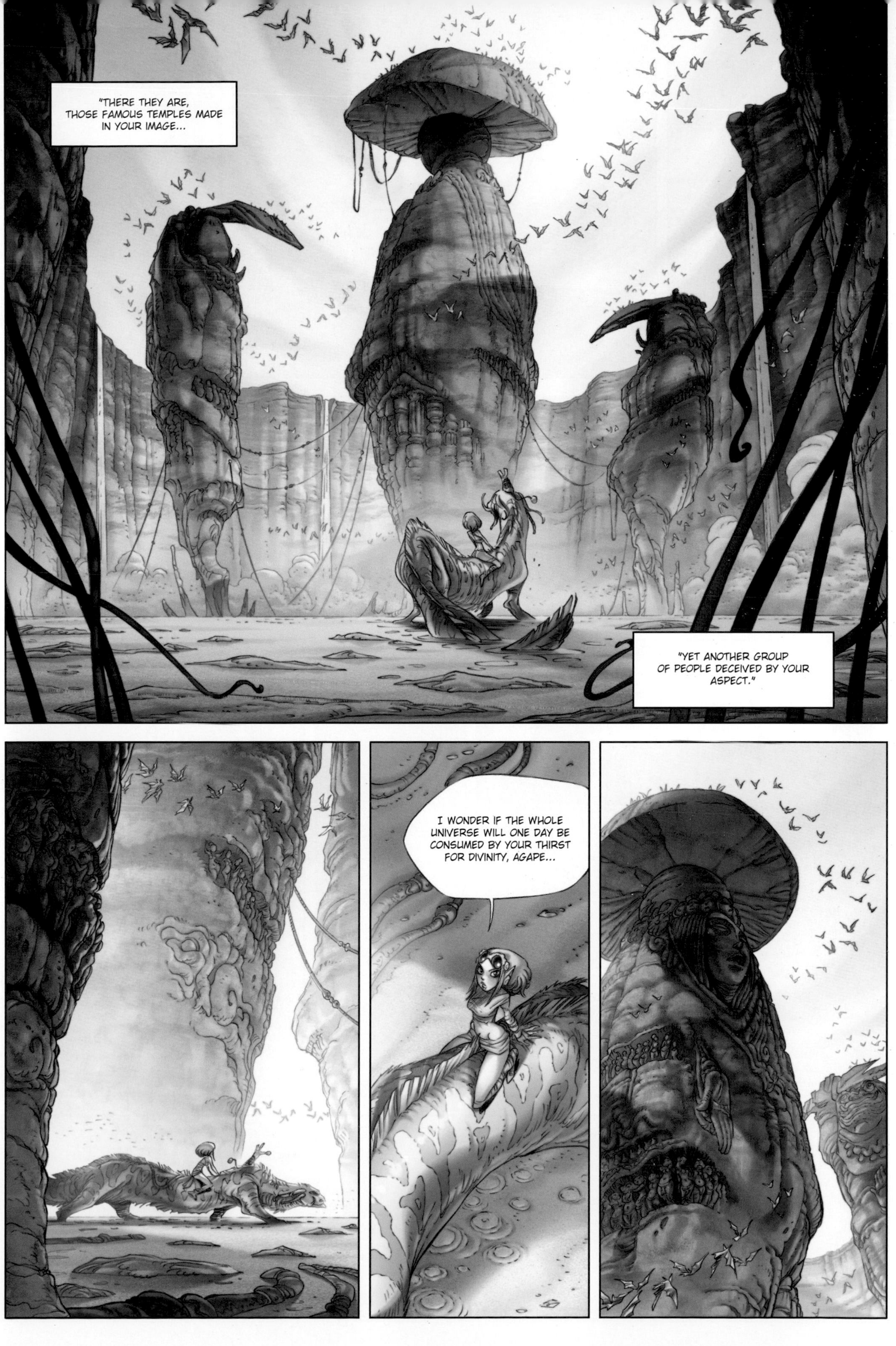
"THERE THEY ARE,
THOSE FAMOUS TEMPLES MADE
IN YOUR IMAGE...
"YET ANOTHER GROUP
OF PEOPLE DECEIVED BY YOUR
ASPECT."
I WONDER IF THE WHOLE
UNIVERSE WILL ONE DAY BE
CONSUMED BY YOUR THIRST
FOR DIVINITY, AGAPE...

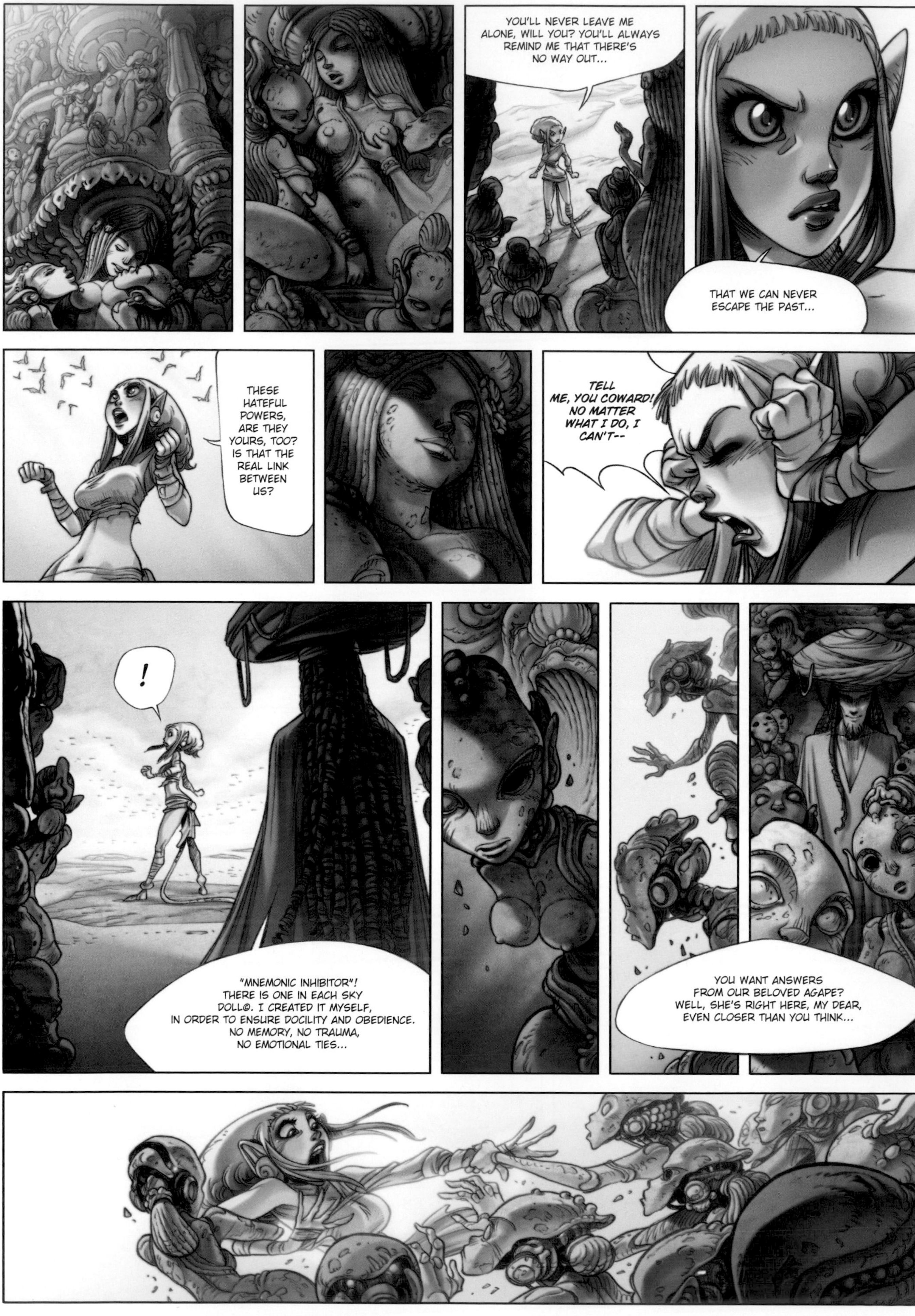
YOU'LL NEVER LEAVE ME ALONE, WILL YOU? YOU'LL ALWAYS REMIND ME THAT THERE'S NO WAY OUT...
THAT WE CAN NEVER ESCAPE THE PAST...
THESE HATEFUL POWERS, ARE THEY YOURS, TOO? IS THAT THE REAL LINK BETWEEN US?
TELL ME, YOU COWARD! NO MATTER WHAT I DO, I CAN'T--
!
"MNEMONIC INHIBITOR"! THERE IS ONE IN EACH SKY DOLL©. I CREATED IT MYSELF, IN ORDER TO ENSURE DOCILITY AND OBEDIENCE. NO MEMORY, NO TRAUMA, NO EMOTIONAL TIES...
YOU WANT ANSWERS FROM OUR BELOVED AGAPE? WELL, SHE'S RIGHT HERE, MY DEAR, EVEN CLOSER THAN YOU THINK...

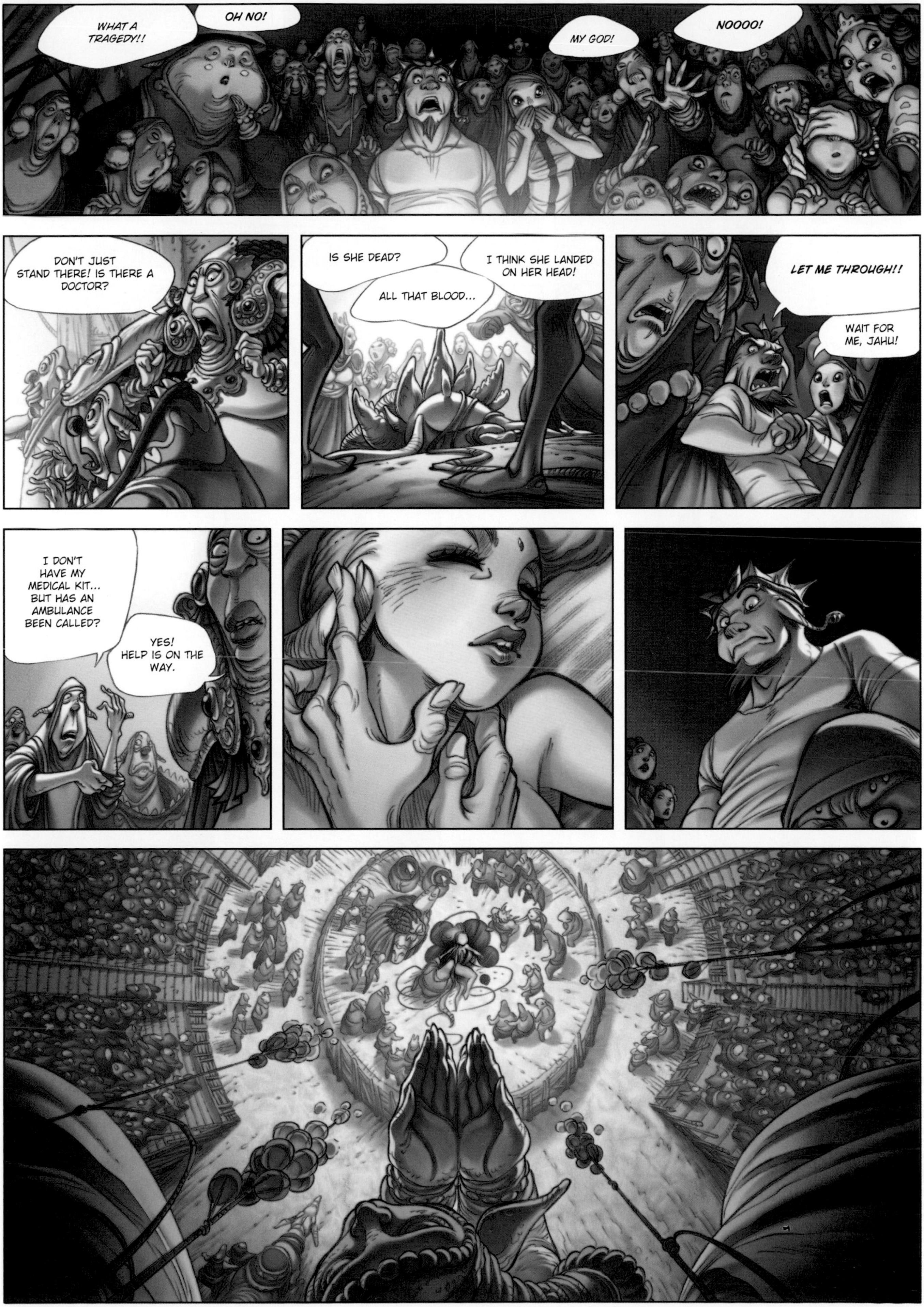
WHAT A TRAGEDY!!
OH NO!
MY GOD!
NOOOO!
DON'T JUST STAND THERE! IS THERE A DOCTOR?
IS SHE DEAD?
ALL THAT BLOOD...
I THINK SHE LANDED ON HER HEAD!
LET ME THROUGH!!
WAIT FOR ME, JAHU!
I DON'T HAVE MY MEDICAL KIT... BUT HAS AN AMBULANCE BEEN CALLED?
YES! HELP IS ON THE WAY.

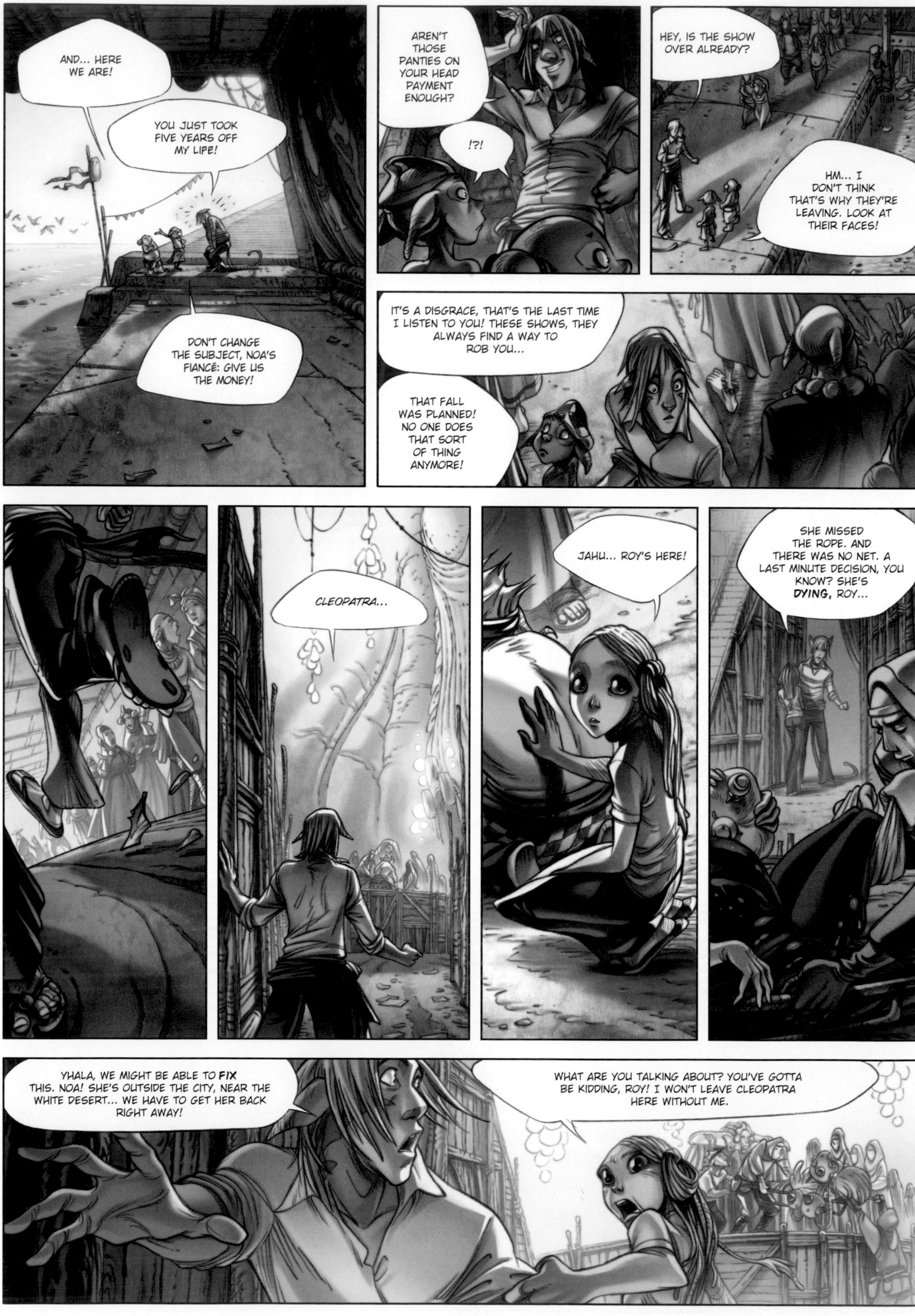
AND... HERE WE ARE!
YOU JUST TOOK FIVE YEARS OFF MY LIFE!
DON'T CHANGE THE SUBJECT, NOA'S FIANCÉ: GIVE US THE MONEY!
AREN'T THOSE PANTIES ON YOUR HEAD PAYMENT ENOUGH?
!?!
HEY, IS THE SHOW OVER ALREADY?
HM... I DON'T THINK THAT'S WHY THEY'RE LEAVING. LOOK AT THEIR FACES!
IT'S A DISGRACE, THAT'S THE LAST TIME I LISTEN TO YOU! THESE SHOWS, THEY ALWAYS FIND A WAY TO ROB YOU...
THAT FALL WAS PLANNED! NO ONE DOES THAT SORT OF THING ANYMORE!
CLEOPATRA...
JAHU... ROY'S HERE!
SHE MISSED THE ROPE. AND THERE WAS NO NET. A LAST MINUTE DECISION, YOU KNOW? SHE'S **DYING**, ROY...
YHALA, WE MIGHT BE ABLE TO **FIX** THIS. NOA! SHE'S OUTSIDE THE CITY, NEAR THE WHITE DESERT... WE HAVE TO GET HER BACK RIGHT AWAY!
WHAT ARE YOU TALKING ABOUT? YOU'VE GOTTA BE KIDDING, ROY! I WON'T LEAVE CLEOPATRA HERE WITHOUT ME.

JAHU, WAIT UP!

THEY SAID THEY HAVE TO OPERATE IMMEDIATELY... I CALLED HER NAME OVER AND OVER.

NOTHING...

ONLY A MIRACLE CAN SAVE HER!

WAIT.... THAT'S WHAT YOU MEANT, ROY! OF COURSE!

SO, WILL YOU COME AND FIND HER WITH ME?

NOA!! WHY DIDN'T I THINK OF IT BEFORE? THAT DOLL COULD RESUSCITATE A ROCK!

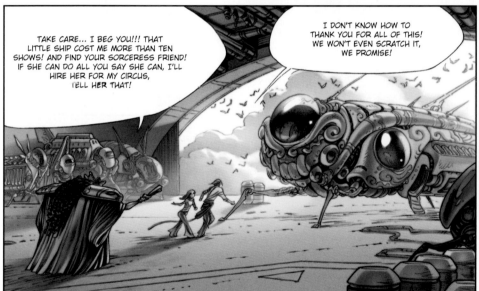

TAKE CARE... I BEG YOU!!! THAT LITTLE SHIP COST ME MORE THAN TEN SHOWS! AND FIND YOUR SORCERESS FRIEND! IF SHE CAN DO ALL YOU SAY SHE CAN, I'LL HIRE HER FOR MY CIRCUS, TELL HER THAT!

I DON'T KNOW HOW TO THANK YOU FOR ALL OF THIS! WE WON'T EVEN SCRATCH IT, WE PROMISE!

CLEOPATRA DYING... AND WE'RE OFF ON THE CHASE YET AGAIN! IGNORANT OF WHAT WE'RE ABOUT TO BE DROPPED INTO ONCE MORE...

...AND NOA'S THE KEY TO IT ALL! NOT MUCH HAS CHANGED IN A YEAR, HEY, YHALA?

THERE IT IS....
NOW I REMEMBER
THE DAY I WAS BORN...

AND YOU WERE THERE!

SO, HERE YOU ARE AGAIN?

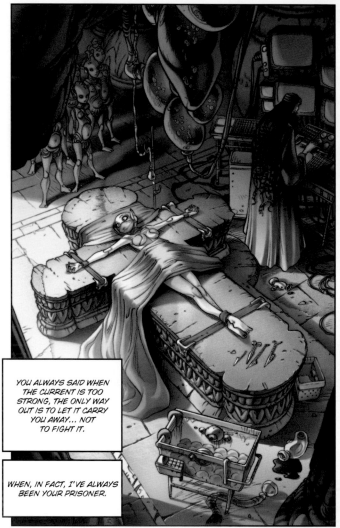

YOU ALWAYS SAID WHEN
THE CURRENT IS TOO
STRONG, THE ONLY WAY
OUT IS TO LET IT CARRY
YOU AWAY... NOT
TO FIGHT IT.

WHEN, IN FACT, I'VE ALWAYS
BEEN YOUR PRISONER.

I HAVE NO MORE
STRENGTH TO FIGHT
YOU, FATHER. IT'S
ALL SO VAGUE...
WHY AM I HERE,
TIED TO THIS
BED AGAIN?

BECAUSE HERE
YOU WILL BE REBORN! DON'T
BE AFRAID...

AGAPE!

ONCE YOU'RE FREE OF THIS PLASTIC
SHELL, YOU'LL REMEMBER, MY SWEET...
YOU, US, YOUR POWER! WHEN YOU AND
LUDOVICA WERE CHOSEN AS THE NEW FACE
OF THE CHURCH, THE COUNCIL WERE
SO PLEASED...

...IN THEIR EYES YOU WOULD BE THE PERFECT
BALANCE TO YOUR SISTER. SHE WOULD HOLD
THE TEMPORAL POWER, AND YOU, THE SPIRITUAL. BUT
YOU WERE... TOO PERFECT! DAY BY DAY,
YOUR POWER GREW...

YOU SPOKE
DIRECTLY TO THE
POOR AND THAT
DISPLEASED THOSE
WHO WANTED YOU ON THE
THRONE. THE PRIESTS'
CONSPIRACY BEGAN.

AND I COULDN'T SEE IT!
I WAS BLINDED BY THE
LIGHT THAT EMANATED FROM YOU.
MY GOD, TO BE BOTH THE
UNTOUCHABLE SAINT AND AN
INSATIABLE ANIMAL!

LIKE ALWAYS,
YOU SAW WHAT WAS
COMING; YOUR AWFUL
ELIMINATION AND THE
PROCLAMATION OF
LUDOVICA AS THE
SOLE PAPESSE...

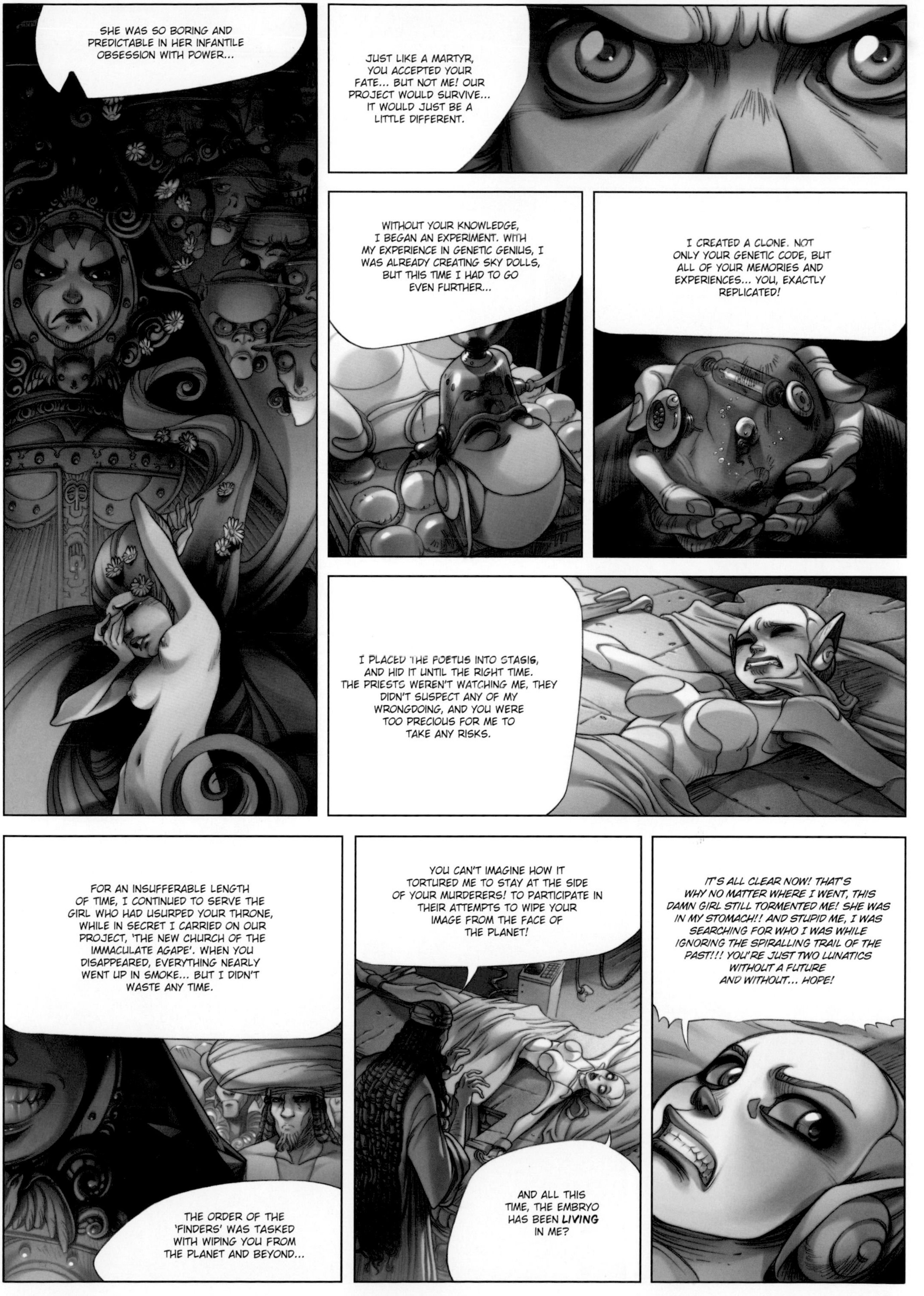
SHE WAS SO BORING AND PREDICTABLE IN HER INFANTILE OBSESSION WITH POWER...
JUST LIKE A MARTYR, YOU ACCEPTED YOUR FATE... BUT NOT ME! OUR PROJECT WOULD SURVIVE... IT WOULD JUST BE A LITTLE DIFFERENT.
WITHOUT YOUR KNOWLEDGE, I BEGAN AN EXPERIMENT. WITH MY EXPERIENCE IN GENETIC GENIUS, I WAS ALREADY CREATING SKY DOLLS, BUT THIS TIME I HAD TO GO EVEN FURTHER...
I CREATED A CLONE. NOT ONLY YOUR GENETIC CODE, BUT ALL OF YOUR MEMORIES AND EXPERIENCES... YOU, EXACTLY REPLICATED!
I PLACED THE FOETUS INTO STASIS, AND HID IT UNTIL THE RIGHT TIME. THE PRIESTS WEREN'T WATCHING ME, THEY DIDN'T SUSPECT ANY OF MY WRONGDOING, AND YOU WERE TOO PRECIOUS FOR ME TO TAKE ANY RISKS.
FOR AN INSUFFERABLE LENGTH OF TIME, I CONTINUED TO SERVE THE GIRL WHO HAD USURPED YOUR THRONE, WHILE IN SECRET I CARRIED ON OUR PROJECT, 'THE NEW CHURCH OF THE IMMACULATE AGAPE'. WHEN YOU DISAPPEARED, EVERYTHING NEARLY WENT UP IN SMOKE... BUT I DIDN'T WASTE ANY TIME.
THE ORDER OF THE 'FINDERS' WAS TASKED WITH WIPING YOU FROM THE PLANET AND BEYOND...
YOU CAN'T IMAGINE HOW IT TORTURED ME TO STAY AT THE SIDE OF YOUR MURDERERS! TO PARTICIPATE IN THEIR ATTEMPTS TO WIPE YOUR IMAGE FROM THE FACE OF THE PLANET!
AND ALL THIS TIME, THE EMBRYO HAS BEEN **LIVING** IN ME?
IT'S ALL CLEAR NOW! THAT'S WHY NO MATTER WHERE I WENT, THIS DAMN GIRL STILL TORMENTED ME! SHE WAS IN MY STOMACH!! AND STUPID ME, I WAS SEARCHING FOR WHO I WAS WHILE IGNORING THE SPIRALLING TRAIL OF THE PAST!!! YOU'RE JUST TWO LUNATICS WITHOUT A FUTURE AND WITHOUT... HOPE!

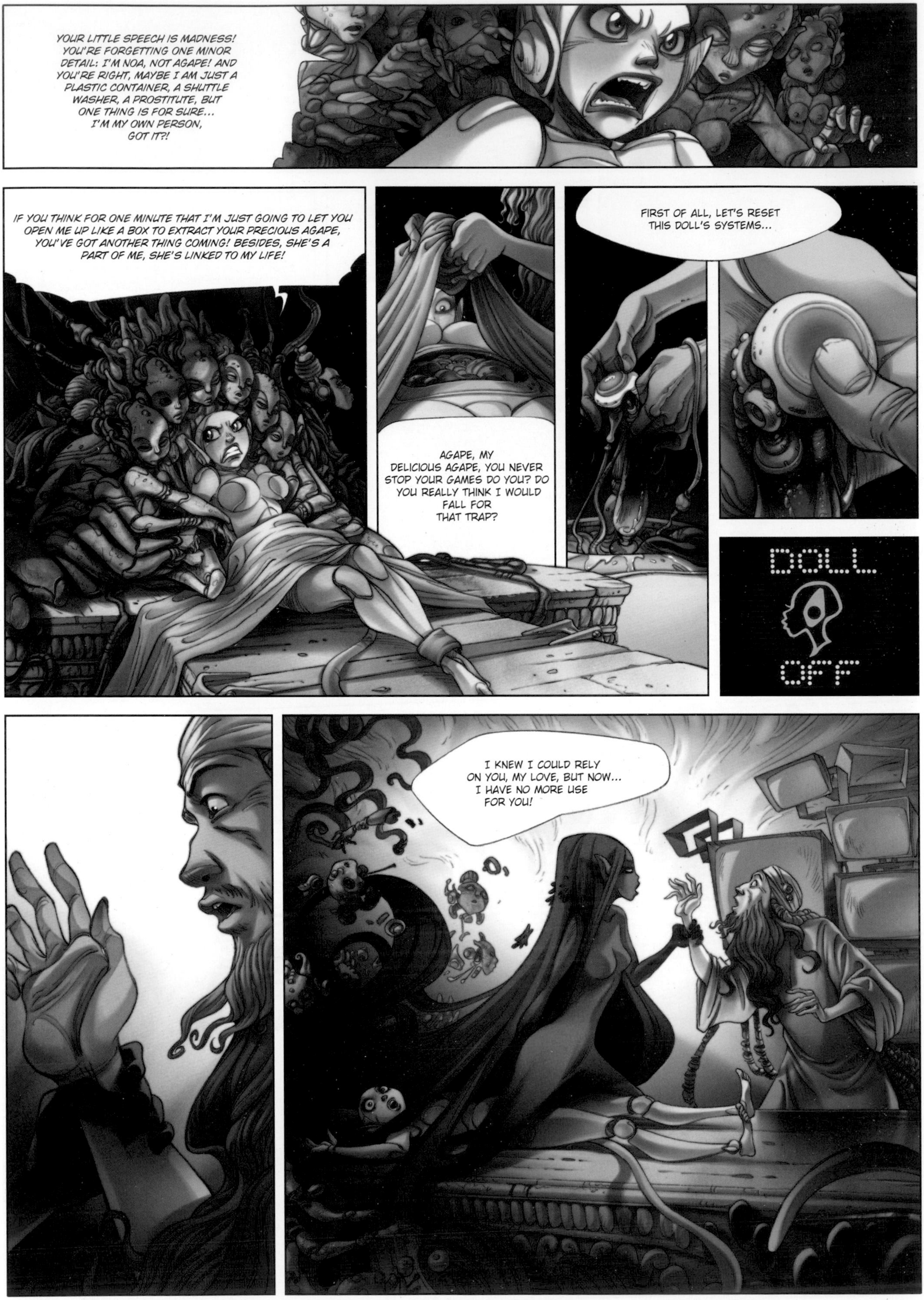
YOUR LITTLE SPEECH IS MADNESS! YOU'RE FORGETTING ONE MINOR DETAIL: I'M NOA, NOT AGAPE! AND YOU'RE RIGHT, MAYBE I AM JUST A PLASTIC CONTAINER, A SHUTTLE WASHER, A PROSTITUTE, BUT ONE THING IS FOR SURE... I'M MY OWN PERSON, GOT IT?!
IF YOU THINK FOR ONE MINUTE THAT I'M JUST GOING TO LET YOU OPEN ME UP LIKE A BOX TO EXTRACT YOUR PRECIOUS AGAPE, YOU'VE GOT ANOTHER THING COMING! BESIDES, SHE'S A PART OF ME, SHE'S LINKED TO MY LIFE!
AGAPE, MY DELICIOUS AGAPE, YOU NEVER STOP YOUR GAMES DO YOU? DO YOU REALLY THINK I WOULD FALL FOR THAT TRAP?
FIRST OF ALL, LET'S RESET THIS DOLL'S SYSTEMS...
DOLL
OFF
I KNEW I COULD RELY ON YOU, MY LOVE, BUT NOW... I HAVE NO MORE USE FOR YOU!

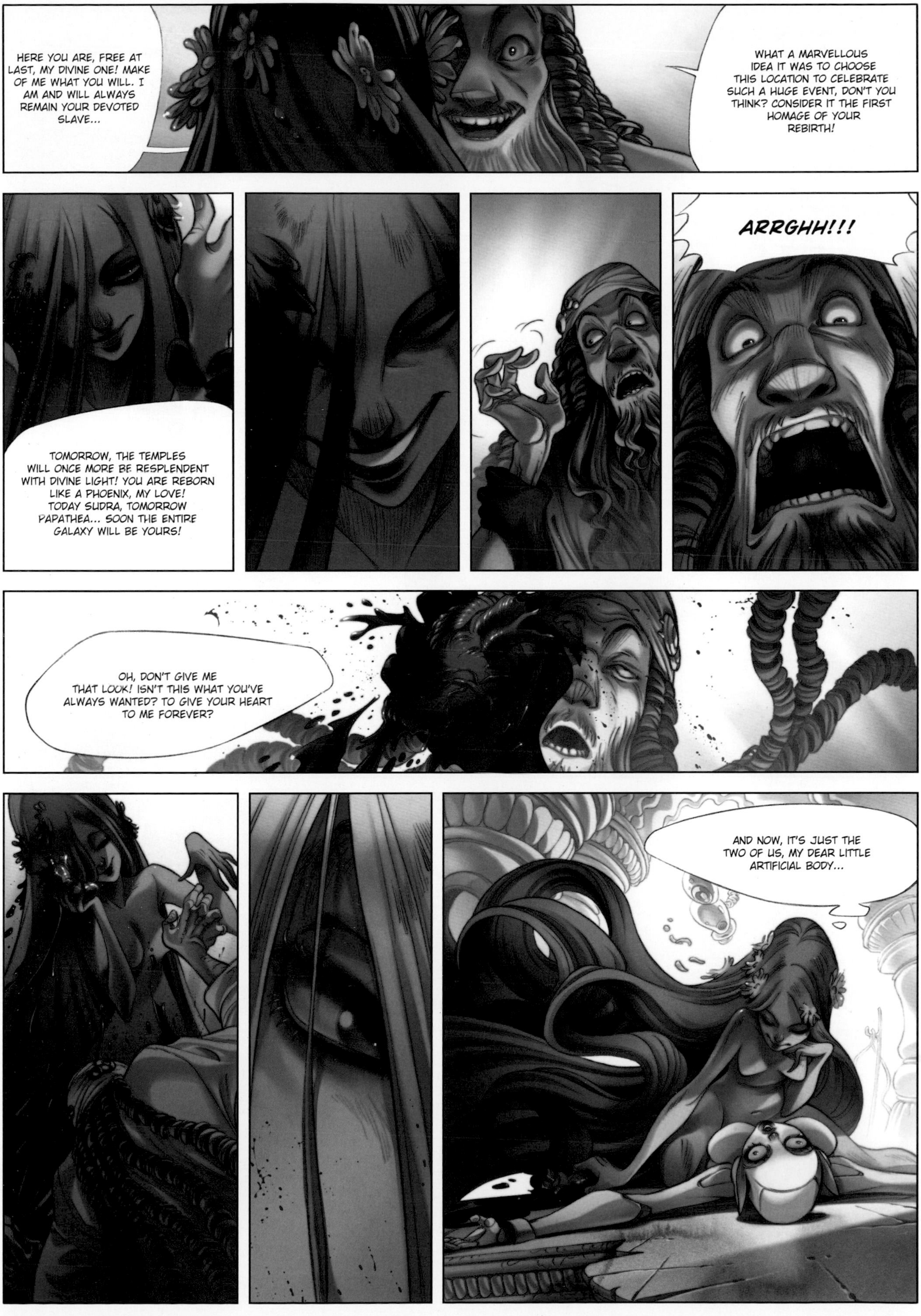
HERE YOU ARE, FREE AT LAST, MY DIVINE ONE! MAKE OF ME WHAT YOU WILL. I AM AND WILL ALWAYS REMAIN YOUR DEVOTED SLAVE...
WHAT A MARVELLOUS IDEA IT WAS TO CHOOSE THIS LOCATION TO CELEBRATE SUCH A HUGE EVENT, DON'T YOU THINK? CONSIDER IT THE FIRST HOMAGE OF YOUR REBIRTH!
TOMORROW, THE TEMPLES WILL ONCE MORE BE RESPLENDENT WITH DIVINE LIGHT! YOU ARE REBORN LIKE A PHOENIX, MY LOVE! TODAY SUDRA, TOMORROW PAPATHEA... SOON THE ENTIRE GALAXY WILL BE YOURS!
ARRGHH!!!
OH, DON'T GIVE ME THAT LOOK! ISN'T THIS WHAT YOU'VE ALWAYS WANTED? TO GIVE YOUR HEART TO ME FOREVER?
AND NOW, IT'S JUST THE TWO OF US, MY DEAR LITTLE ARTIFICIAL BODY...

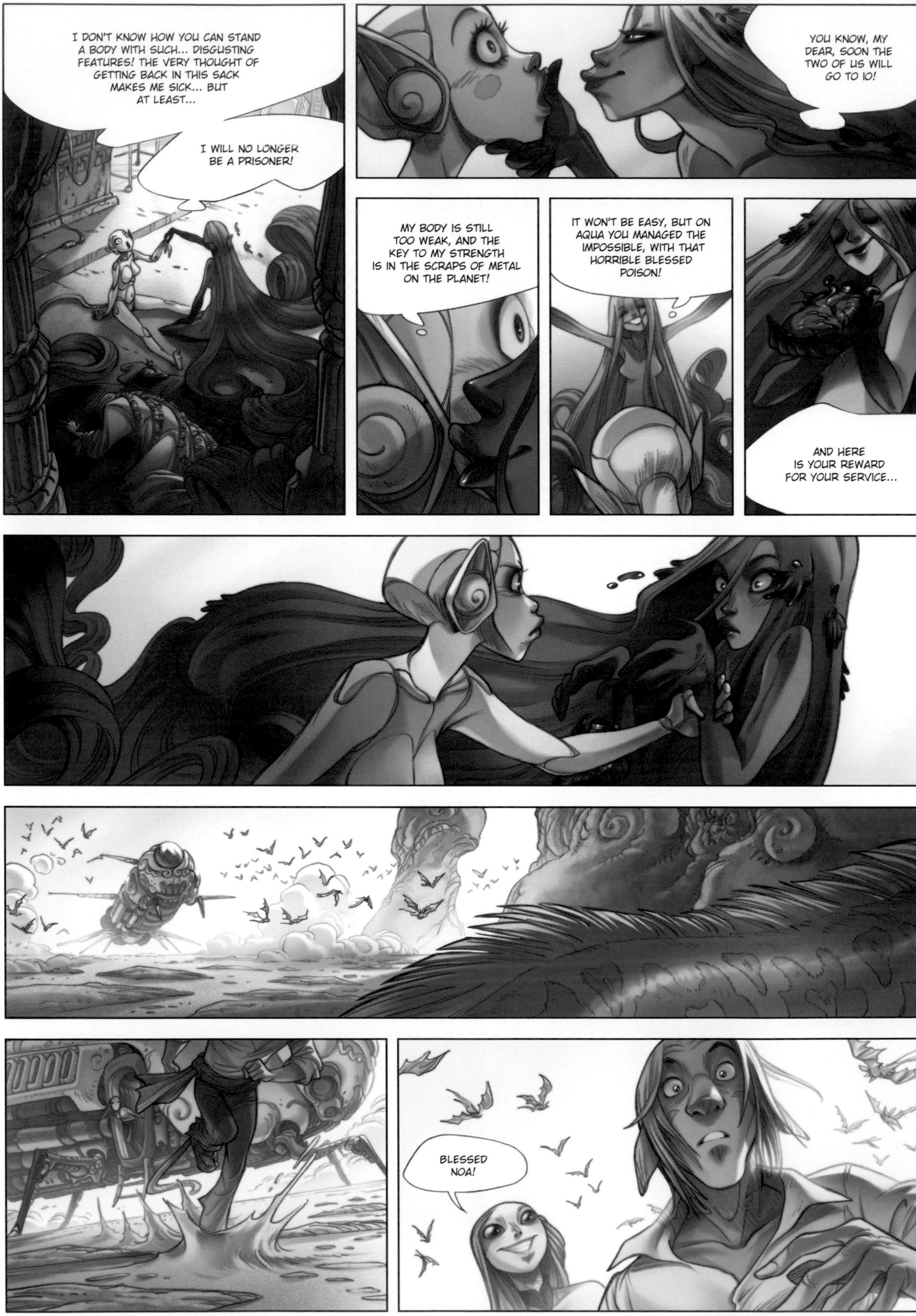
I DON'T KNOW HOW YOU CAN STAND A BODY WITH SUCH... DISGUSTING FEATURES! THE VERY THOUGHT OF GETTING BACK IN THIS SACK MAKES ME SICK... BUT AT LEAST...
I WILL NO LONGER BE A PRISONER!
YOU KNOW, MY DEAR, SOON THE TWO OF US WILL GO TO IO!
MY BODY IS STILL TOO WEAK, AND THE KEY TO MY STRENGTH IS IN THE SCRAPS OF METAL ON THE PLANET!
IT WON'T BE EASY, BUT ON AQUA YOU MANAGED THE IMPOSSIBLE, WITH THAT HORRIBLE BLESSED POISON!
AND HERE IS YOUR REWARD FOR YOUR SERVICE...
BLESSED NOA!

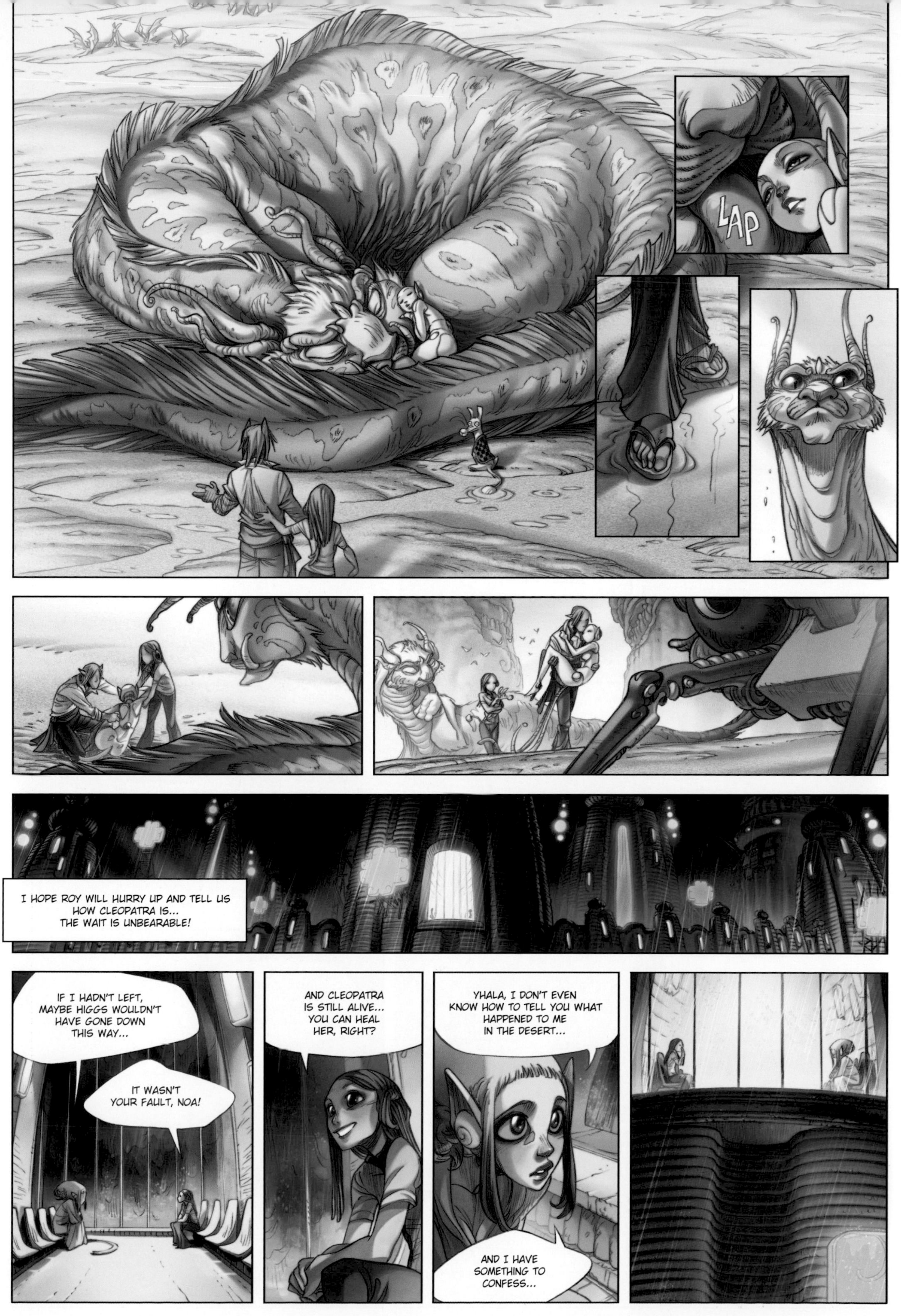
LAP
I HOPE ROY WILL HURRY UP AND TELL US HOW CLEOPATRA IS... THE WAIT IS UNBEARABLE!
IF I HADN'T LEFT, MAYBE HIGGS WOULDN'T HAVE GONE DOWN THIS WAY...
IT WASN'T YOUR FAULT, NOA!
AND CLEOPATRA IS STILL ALIVE... YOU CAN HEAL HER, RIGHT?
YHALA, I DON'T EVEN KNOW HOW TO TELL YOU WHAT HAPPENED TO ME IN THE DESERT...
AND I HAVE SOMETHING TO CONFESS...

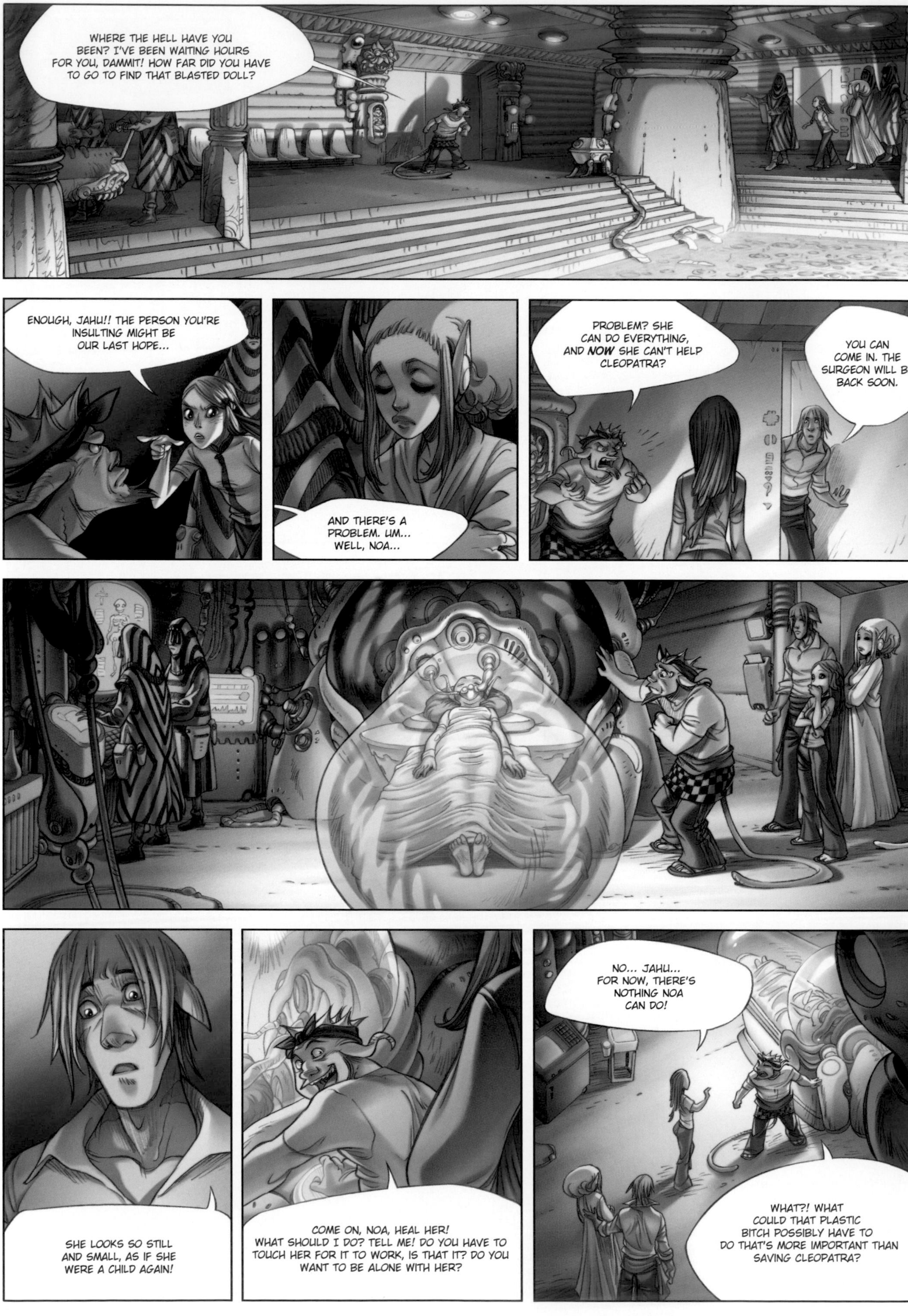
WHERE THE HELL HAVE YOU BEEN? I'VE BEEN WAITING HOURS FOR YOU, DAMMIT! HOW FAR DID YOU HAVE TO GO TO FIND THAT BLASTED DOLL?
ENOUGH, JAHU!! THE PERSON YOU'RE INSULTING MIGHT BE OUR LAST HOPE...
AND THERE'S A PROBLEM. UM... WELL, NOA...
PROBLEM? SHE CAN DO EVERYTHING, AND NOW SHE CAN'T HELP CLEOPATRA?
YOU CAN COME IN. THE SURGEON WILL BE BACK SOON.
SHE LOOKS SO STILL AND SMALL, AS IF SHE WERE A CHILD AGAIN!
COME ON, NOA, HEAL HER! WHAT SHOULD I DO? TELL ME! DO YOU HAVE TO TOUCH HER FOR IT TO WORK, IS THAT IT? DO YOU WANT TO BE ALONE WITH HER?
NO... JAHU... FOR NOW, THERE'S NOTHING NOA CAN DO!
WHAT?! WHAT COULD THAT PLASTIC BITCH POSSIBLY HAVE TO DO THAT'S MORE IMPORTANT THAN SAVING CLEOPATRA?

IS THIS A JOKE?! YOU'RE NOT GOING ANYWHERE! YOU BRING HER BACK TO ME, YOU HEAR? RIGHT NOW!

IO? THE PLANET OF BROKEN ROBOTS, EACH ONE AS MAD AS THE NEXT?

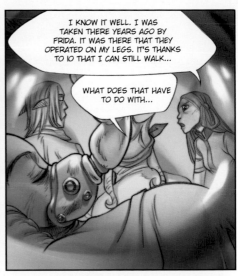

I KNOW IT WELL. I WAS TAKEN THERE YEARS AGO BY FRIDA. IT WAS THERE THAT THEY OPERATED ON MY LEGS. IT'S THANKS TO IO THAT I CAN STILL WALK...

WHAT DOES THAT HAVE TO DO WITH...

NOA HAS TO GO TO IO, AND I'M GOING WITH HER...

I DON'T HAVE POWERS ANYMORE, JAHU. I LOST THEM. IO IS THE ONLY CHANCE TO GET THEM BACK...

WHAT ARE YOU TALKING ABOUT? I KNOW YOU WERE DOING MIRACLES RIGHT UP UNTIL YESTERDAY!

FOR NOW, I CAN'T EXPLAIN ROY... BUT YOU HAVE TO BELIEVE ME!

BELIEVE YOU? JUST LIKE THAT? WHY CAN'T YOU JUST TELL THE TRUTH FOR ONCE IN YOUR STUPID LIFE?

JAHU...

CAN I REMIND YOU WHY WE'RE EVEN ON THIS PLANET? WE'RE FUGITIVES... OUTCASTS! BECAUSE OF THIS BITCH! AND NOW, WHEN SHE COULD BE USEFUL FOR ONCE, SHE RUNS OFF TO I DON'T EVEN KNOW WHERE!

I'M SORRY... I'M SO SORRY!

GET BACK HERE! YOU'LL HAVE CLEOPATRA ON YOUR CONSCIENCE FOREVER... IF YOU EVEN HAVE ONE!

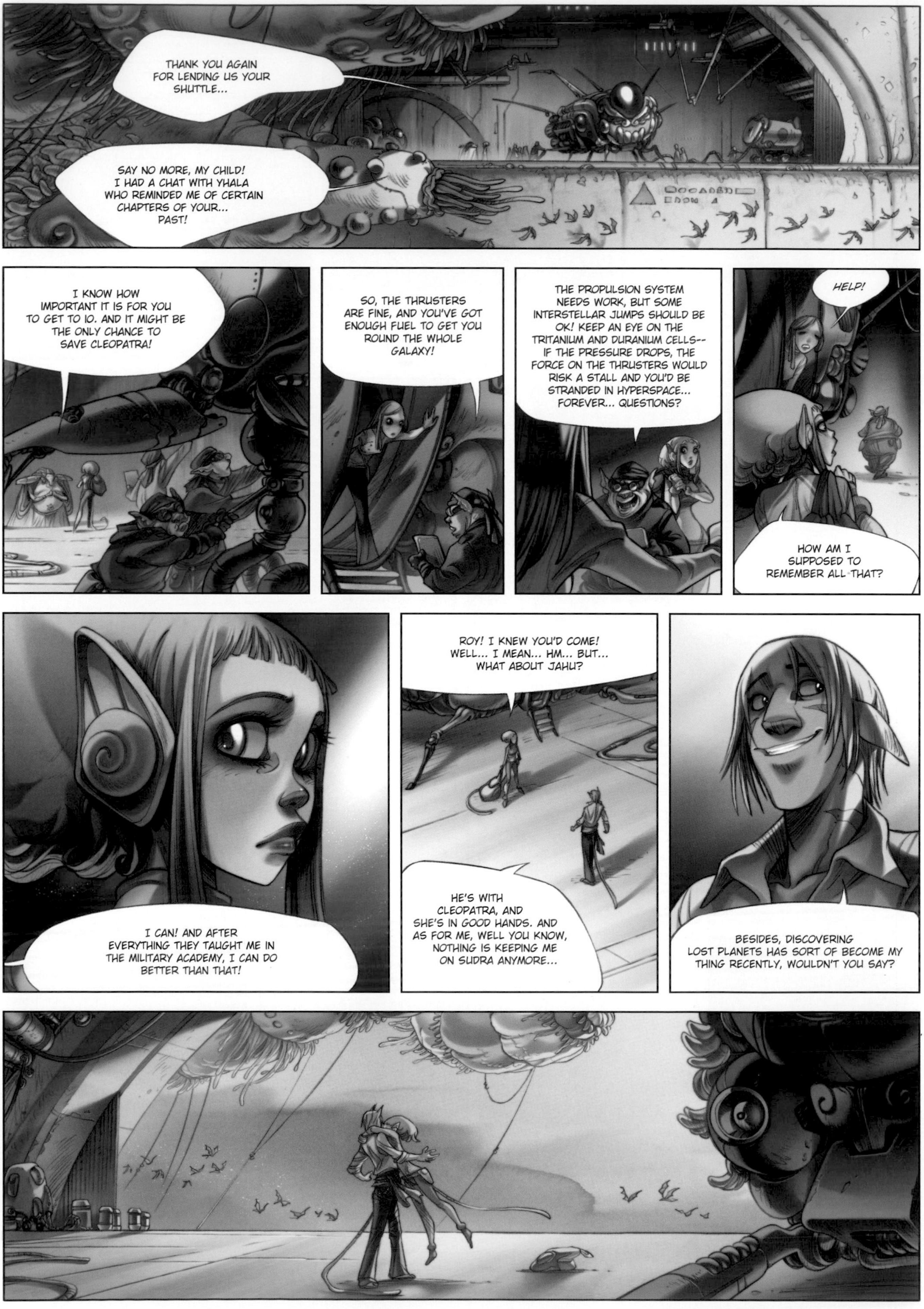
THANK YOU AGAIN FOR LENDING US YOUR SHUTTLE...
SAY NO MORE, MY CHILD! I HAD A CHAT WITH YHALA WHO REMINDED ME OF CERTAIN CHAPTERS OF YOUR... PAST!
I KNOW HOW IMPORTANT IT IS FOR YOU TO GET TO IO. AND IT MIGHT BE THE ONLY CHANCE TO SAVE CLEOPATRA!
SO, THE THRUSTERS ARE FINE, AND YOU'VE GOT ENOUGH FUEL TO GET YOU ROUND THE WHOLE GALAXY!
THE PROPULSION SYSTEM NEEDS WORK, BUT SOME INTERSTELLAR JUMPS SHOULD BE OK! KEEP AN EYE ON THE TRITANIUM AND DURANIUM CELLS-- IF THE PRESSURE DROPS, THE FORCE ON THE THRUSTERS WOULD RISK A STALL AND YOU'D BE STRANDED IN HYPERSPACE... FOREVER... QUESTIONS?
HELP!
HOW AM I SUPPOSED TO REMEMBER ALL THAT?
I CAN! AND AFTER EVERYTHING THEY TAUGHT ME IN THE MILITARY ACADEMY, I CAN DO BETTER THAN THAT!
ROY! I KNEW YOU'D COME! WELL... I MEAN... HM... BUT... WHAT ABOUT JAHU?
HE'S WITH CLEOPATRA, AND SHE'S IN GOOD HANDS. AND AS FOR ME, WELL YOU KNOW, NOTHING IS KEEPING ME ON SUDRA ANYMORE...
BESIDES, DISCOVERING LOST PLANETS HAS SORT OF BECOME MY THING RECENTLY, WOULDN'T YOU SAY?

THE END...

Barbucci Canepa

SKY·DOLL

4 Sudra

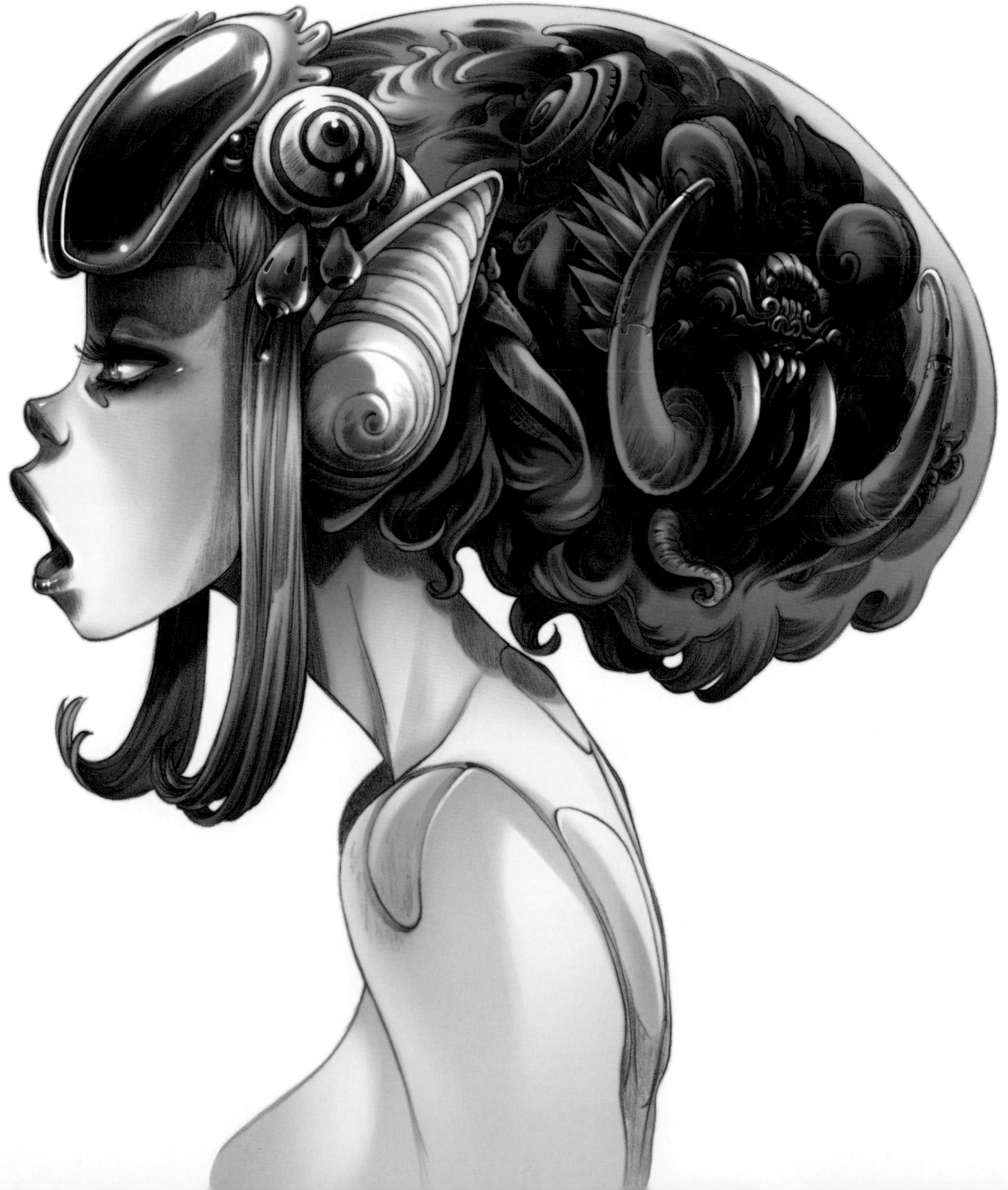

SKY·DOLL

COVER GALLERY

ISSUE 1

Barbucci
Canepa
SKY·DOLL
Sudra
TITAN COMICS
$3.99
2017
ISSUE #01
SUGGESTED FOR MATURE READERS

COVER A BY BARBUCCI & CANEPA

Barbucci
Canepa
SKY·DOLL
Sudra
TITAN COMICS
$3.99
2017
ISSUE #01
SUGGESTED FOR MATURE READERS

COVER B BY BARBUCCI & CANEPA

TITAN COMICS
$3.99
2017
ISSUE #01
SUGGESTED FOR MATURE READERS
Barbucci
Canepa
SKY·DOLL
Sudra

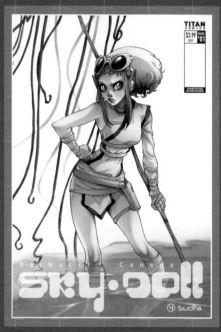

COVER C BY BARBUCCI & CANEPA

Barbucci
Canepa
SKY·DOLL
TITAN COMICS
$3.99
2017
ISSUE #01
SUGGESTED FOR MATURE READERS

COVER D BY BARBUCCI & CANEPA

Barbucci
Canepa
SKY·DOLL
Sudra
TITAN COMICS
$3.99
2017
ISSUE #01
SUGGESTED FOR MATURE READERS

COVER E BY MATTEO DE LONGIS

ISSUE 2

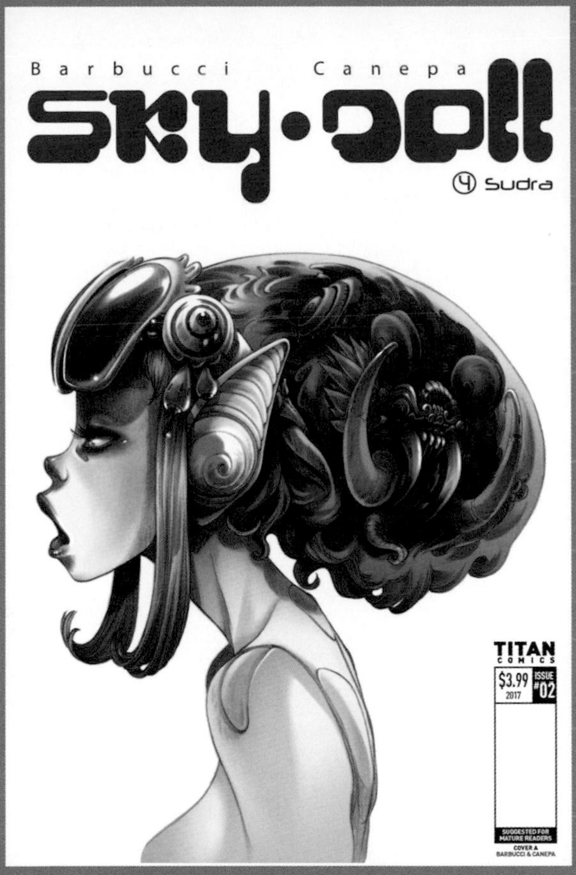
Barbucci Canepa
SKY·DOLL
4 Sudra
TITAN COMICS
$3.99 2017
ISSUE #02
SUGGESTED FOR MATURE READERS
COVER A BARBUCCI & CANEPA

COVER A BY BARBUCCI & CANEPA

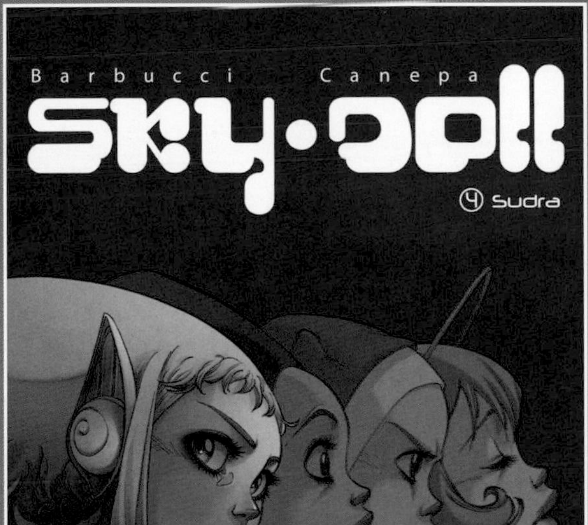
Barbucci Canepa
SKY·DOLL
4 Sudra
TITAN
$3.99 2017
ISSUE #02
SUGGESTED FOR MATURE READERS

COVER B BY BARBUCCI & CANEPA

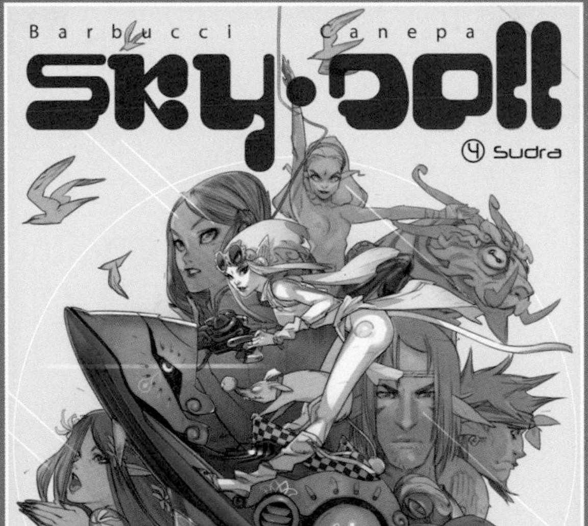
Barbucci Canepa
SKY·DOLL
4 Sudra
TITAN COMICS
$3.99 2017
ISSUE #02
SUGGESTED FOR MATURE READERS
COVER C MATTEO DE LONGIS

COVER C BY MATTEO DE LONGIS

Sky·Doll

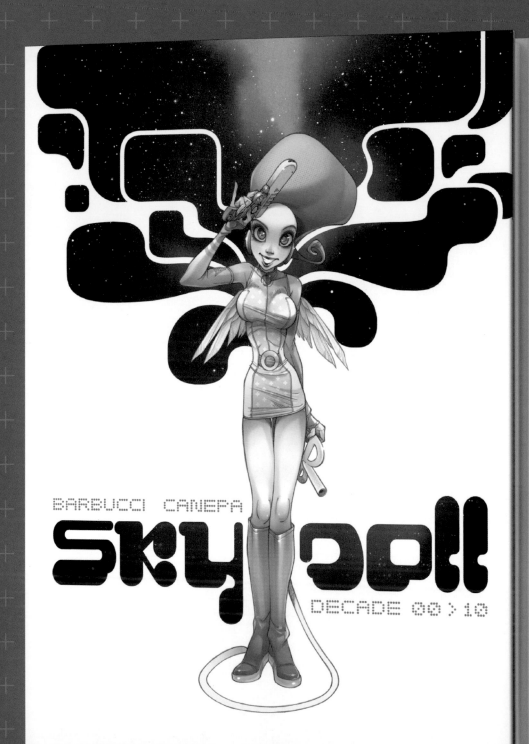

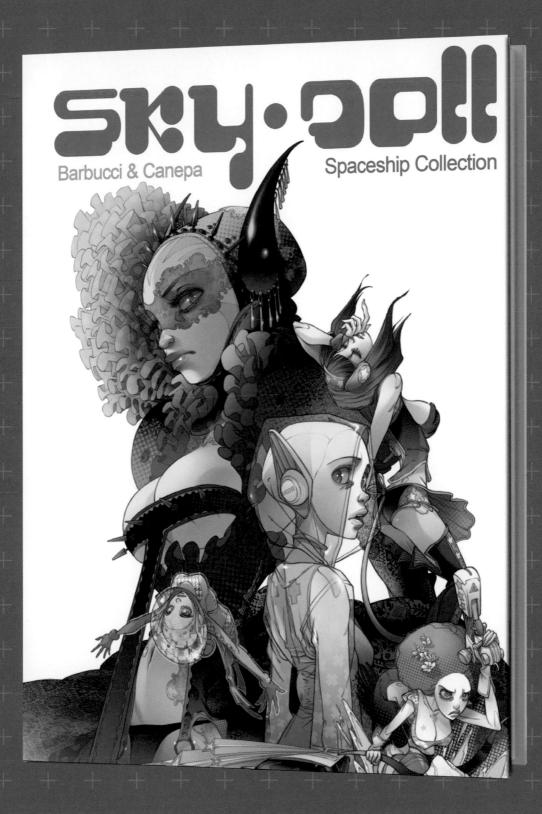

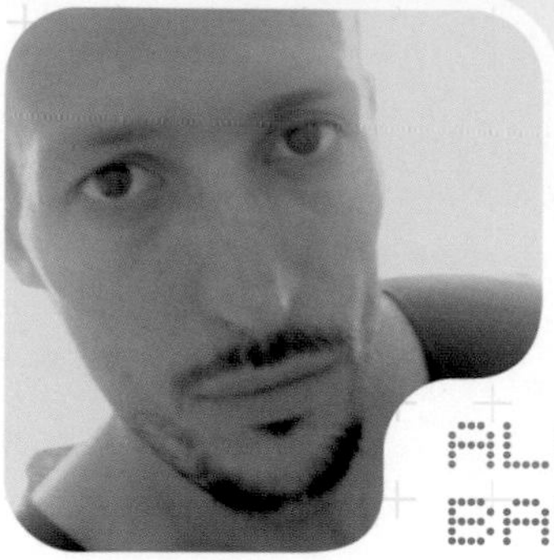

ALESSANDRO BARBUCCI

...was born in 1973 in Genoa, Italy. From the age of 18 he began to explore the world of comic books: within his first ten years in the industry he had drawn around 1200 pages, mostly for **Disney Editorial**. His contributions on numerous creative projects ranged from storyboarding to animation and directing. Until 1999, he taught comic art techniques at the Disney Academy in Milan.

In 1997, Alessandro created (along with Barbara Canepa) the universe and characters of the *W.I.T.C.H* series, a project which, since 2001, has experienced immense international success and has been published in over 100 countries.

That same year, the two created the science-fiction saga *Skydoll*, published by **Soleil** and distributed throughout Europe; and more recently in Korea, Japan and the USA by **Marvel Comics**. Lauded by critics and the public alike, the series won several awards including; "Best Series of the Year," "Best Art and Colors," and "The Albert Uderzo Prize for Young Talent." Its success even extended to Paris art galleries, who regularly exhibit original artwork.

Alessandro and Barbara are also the graphic designers on *Monster Allergy*, a comic for children published in March 2003 by Soleil in France, and distributed around the world. It too has won several awards: "Best Children's Comic" in Italy, France and Germany, and the series was made into a TV show in January 2006. Produced by **Rainbow, Futurikon** and **Disney Channel**, *Monster Allergy* was the first European comic to be bought by **Warner Brothers** America and currently airs on **Cartoon Network**.

In 2010, Alessandro re-joined the world of animation: writing a TV series for young audiences. He also collaborated on the comic *Lord Burger* (story by Arleston and Alwett, published by **Glenat**), in which he took over character designs and art after Volume 3.

Finally, in 2010, Alessandro published the first two volumes of a new series that he had written and drawn: *Chosp: Power to the Flies*. He is also now working on the fantasy series *Ekho: Mirrored World*.

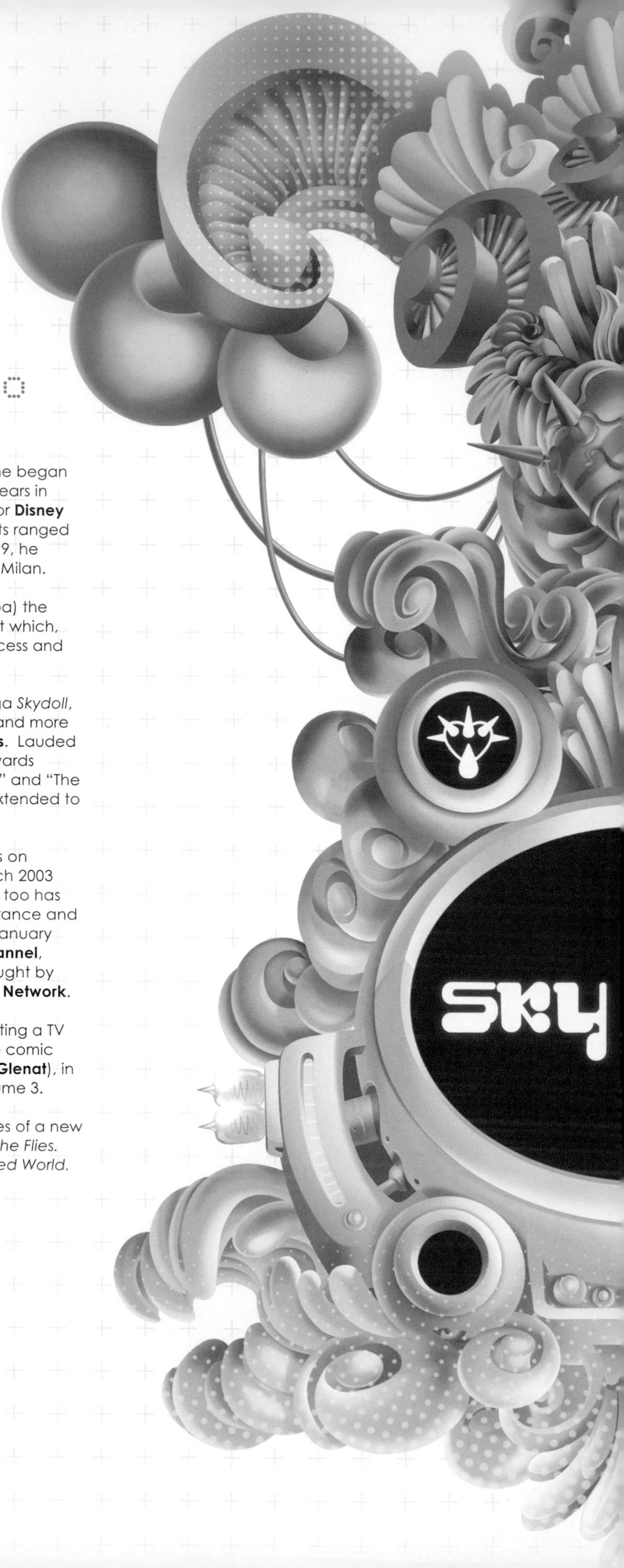
SKY

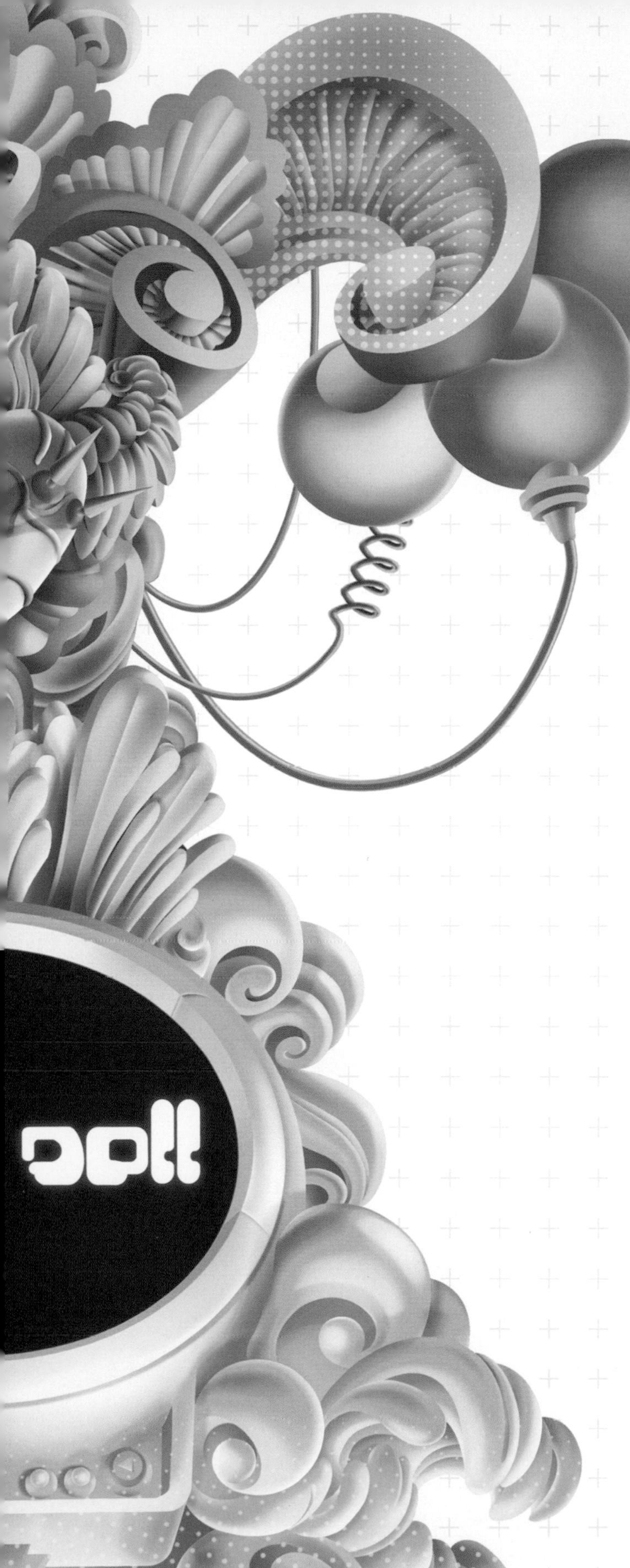
doll

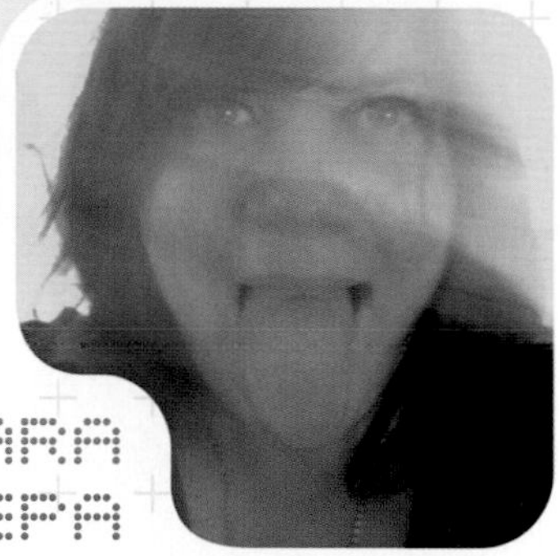

BARBARA CANEPA

... was born in 1969 in Genoa, Italy. After her studies at the Faculty of Architecture in the University of Genoa, she worked as an illustrator, notably in advertising. In 1996, **Disney** opened its doors to her, offering her the job of illustrating books and magazine. Up until 2002, she drew stories and covers for *The Little Mermaid* magazine, while attending 'pictorial techniques' classes at the Disney Academy. There were exhibitions of her oil paintings in both Italy and the United States. She collaborated on numerous creative projects for Disney as both a character designer and artist, working together with Alessandro Barbucci to create comic strips and illustrations for the magazine's press.

First collaborating in 1997, they created the concept, characters, backgrounds, graphic style, and color pallet of a new magazine, *W.I.T.C.H.* Since 2001, its success has been considerable: published around the world, and winner of several awards, *W.I.T.C.H* has now sold over 50 million copies.

Barbara is now an Editor at **Soleil**. She is in charge of several prestigious collections: *Métamorphose* and *Venusdea*. These collections are famous for offering freedom of expression to those with a background in the arts (such as photographers, designers, illustrators, and pop Surrealist artists).

Several exhibitions of her work took place in late 2010/early 2011, linking her personal projects (*Skydoll, End*) with the two collections she has helped put together for Soleil. She has also curated work by the artists of *Venusdea* and *Métamorphose* in European galleries.

Since finishing this volume, Barbara Canepa has been working on the scripts for her new comic series, *End*, with art by Anna Merli, as well as a novel inspired by her personal life...

Story :
Alessandro Barbucci and Barbara Canepa
Art:
Alessandro Barbucci
Colors:
Barbara Canepa
in collaboration with Cyrille Bertin

Translation:
Jessica Burton

Editor:
Lizzie Kaye

Senior Comics Editor:
Andrew James

Assistant Editors:
Lauren McPhee & Lauren Bowes

Senior Designer:
Andrew Leung

SKY DOLL: SUDRA COLLECTION
ISBN: 9781785861291

First Published in French as SKY DOLL 4: SUDRA. Published August 2017 by Titan Comics, a division of Titan Publishing Group, Ltd.
144 Southwark Street, London SE1 0UP.

10 9 8 7 6 5 4 3 2 1
Printed in China, Titan Comics,

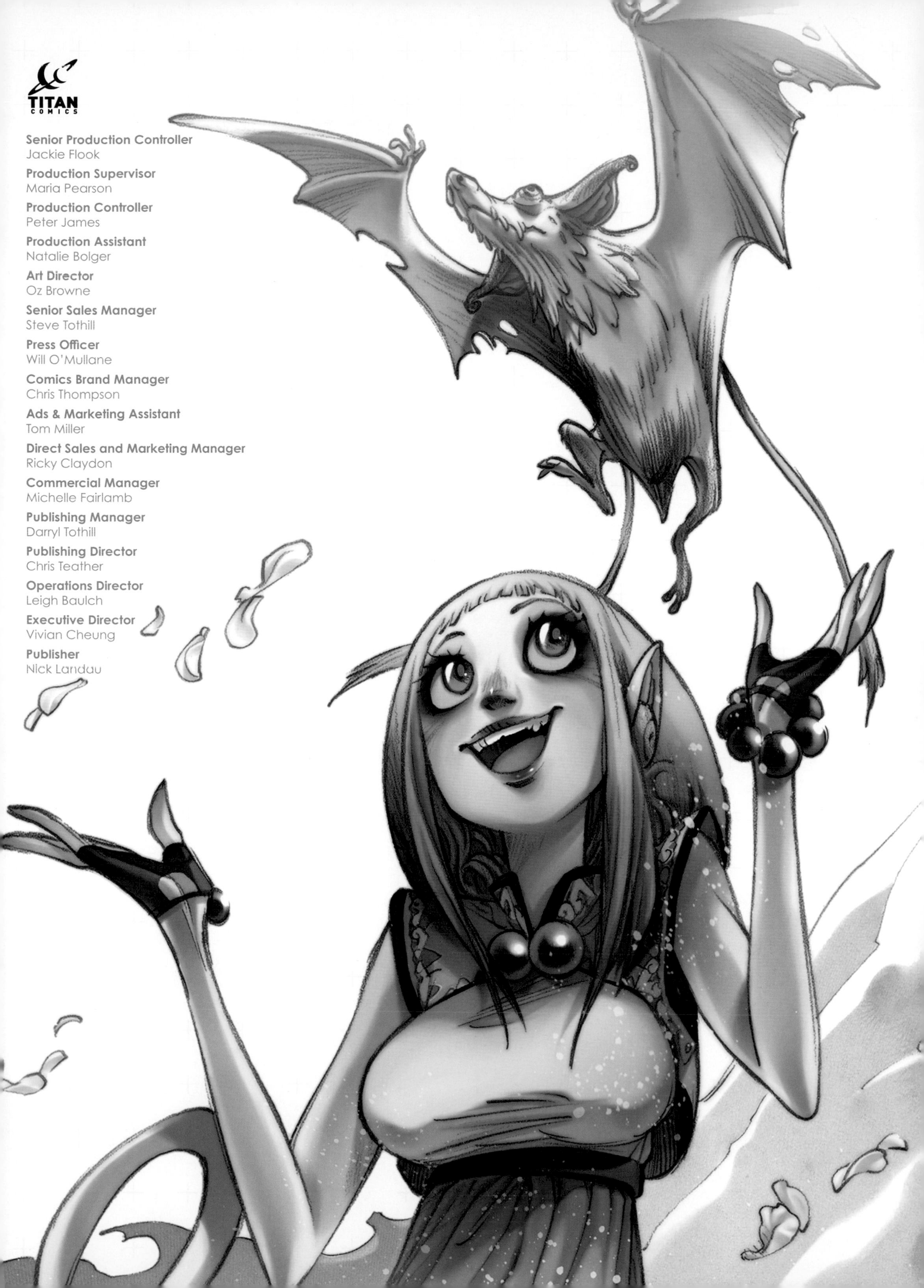

TITAN COMICS

Senior Production Controller
Jackie Flook

Production Supervisor
Maria Pearson

Production Controller
Peter James

Production Assistant
Natalie Bolger

Art Director
Oz Browne

Senior Sales Manager
Steve Tothill

Press Officer
Will O'Mullane

Comics Brand Manager
Chris Thompson

Ads & Marketing Assistant
Tom Miller

Direct Sales and Marketing Manager
Ricky Claydon

Commercial Manager
Michelle Fairlamb

Publishing Manager
Darryl Tothill

Publishing Director
Chris Teather

Operations Director
Leigh Baulch

Executive Director
Vivian Cheung

Publisher
Nick Landau

• Acknowledgements •

Thanks to all those who had the patience to wait for the rest of this story.
All things come to those who wait. (Violet Fane)
Alessandro

I would like to thank:
My familly, who never let me down, who never stumbled, and who taught me to always live with a smile on my face.
All the friends who have always believed in me, who have motivated me, helped me, in particular Jean-Luc, Julien, Kitty, Lucia, Renata and Isabella.
Clotilde, as always, you were the only one who could assist me in this long trial, my friend.
Andrea Cagol, yet again, you were there when I needed you.
Angela and Flavia, my colour wizards.
Jean Wacquet, because you waited all these years, in the dark, patiently, never doubting that this day would finally come.
Cyrille Bertin, the patience and perseverance you had for me to finish this book was without limit. Thank you.
Finally, thank you to Guillaume, who managed to add melody and colour to the world around me...
Barbara

To Barbara and Alessandro for trusting me.
To Sterenn, Lou and Nino...